The Harada Method

the Spirit of Self-Reliance

2nd Edition

Takashi Harada

Norman Bodek

PCS PRESS
Seattle, Washington

Copyrighted ©2012 by the Harada Institute of Education & PCS Inc. (Norman Bodek) All Rights Reserved.

No part of this book may be reproduced or transmitted in any form by any means, electronic or mechanical, including photocopying, recording, or by any information storage and retrieval system without permission in writing from the Publisher.

Publisher's Cataloging-in-Publication data

Names: Harada, Takashi, author. | Bodek, Norman, author.

Title: The Harada method : the spirit of self reliance, 2nd edition / Takashi Harada and Norman Bodek.

Description: Includes bibliographical references and index. | Seattle, WA: PCS Press (Perfect Customer Service, Inc.), 2024.

Identifiers: LCCN: 2024930356 | ISBN: 978-0-9845565-9-5 (hardcover) | 979-8-9872585-9-0 (paperback) | 979-8-9872585-2-1 (ebook)
Subjects: LCSH Performance. | Industrial management. | Organizational behavior. | Organizational change. | Leadership. | Success in business. | BISAC BUSINESS & ECONOMICS / Industrial Management | BUSINESS & ECONOMICS / Organizational Behavior
Classification: LCC HD58.7 .H37 2024 | DDC 658.3--dc23

Printed in the United States of America

1. Human development. 2. Industrial Management. 3. Organizational change. 4. Organizational behavior. 5. Human relations.

P C S Press
1420 5TH AVE, STE 4200
Seattle, WA 98101
info@pcspress.com
www.pcspress.com
Seattle, Washington

Translated by Keiko Morimoto
Edited by Will Hutchens and Beth Simone
Layout by Alicia Katz Pollock
The cover is a stereogram designed by Gene Levine

COVER

The Dragon

The Cover: The picture on the cover is a stereogram: hidden is a three-dimensional picture (3-D) by the artist Gene Levine. If you relax your eyes, focus six inches beyond the top of the book, or look at the blank space above the picture, or hold the cover to your nose and slowly move the page away, you should see this wonderful image emerge.

The picture is Mr. Harada surrounded by dragons. In the Orient, 2012 is the year of the Dragon. Dragons are often held to have major spiritual significance in various religions and cultures around the world. They are associated with wisdom – often said to be wiser than humans – and longevity. In some traditions dragons are said to have taught humans to talk.

Acknowledgments

I want to thank Shigehiro Nakamura, consultant, teacher, Japan Management Association, for introducing me to the Harada Method. I am indebted to Keiko Morimoto, staff member at the Harada Institute, for translating Japanese to English the parts written by Mr. Harada. Noriko Hosoyamada, Kevin Tame, Junwoo Park, David Hubbard, and Udai Hoshi did additional translations. I want to thank all of my students at Portland State University in my Japanese Management class who allowed me to introduce them to the Harada Method, and also to the managers and consultants from industry that took my Harada Method certification class. I am grateful for the fine editing done by Will Hutchens and Beth Simone and the computer work done by Guochao Zhang. I also thank Mark Graban and many others for helping me to inform their audiences about the Harada Method. I thank Karl Wadensten of VIBCO, Inc. for calling me the Godfather of Lean.

I'm gonna make him a Harada Method he can't refuse

By Shmuel (Sam) Korb

Testimonials

"The Harada method is the most powerful system for people development. What sets it apart? It is the focus on building your character while at the same time helping you achieve success. You set a goal and become a new person, the person who you must be to achieve that goal. It's an amazing journey of self-discovery, discipline, and achievement. I was thrilled to be introduced to this by Norman Bodek in 2012. Later, having visited Japan with other CEOs, I met with Takashi Harada. We took part in several workshops and then visited Kobe Mazda. This company achieved great success having implemented Harada's system throughout their organization. It occurred to me that his method is just as powerful for an individual or an organization. Shohei Ohtani – a Japanese high-school baseball player at the time – used this method to later become a pitcher and designated hitter in the major leagues. Today, he is known as the best player in the world. Imagine having a clear goal in your life as well as understanding your purpose and changing each day for the better. I have personally been receiving the benefits of the Harada method for the past ten years. As a leadership excellence coach, I am pleased when my clients summarize their feedback on the method. If I had to sum it up in one sentence it would be, the Harada method is like a gravitational pull towards a better future for everyone, both in and outside of your organization."

   – George Trachilis, P.Eng., President & Coach,
     Leadership Excellence Institute

"We were introduced to the Harada method through George Trachilis, our leadership-excellence coach and consultant. Excited about the direction of our continuous improvement initiatives combined with our desire to improve the experience of our workforce, we embraced the people side of lean and started our self-reliance journey. The stories, professional case studies and personal examples described in this book are more than a "how to" guide. They are inspiring and compelling our teams onward

in the journey to learn and coach others in self-reliance. The Harada Method's four aspects of self-reliance – spirit, skill, physical condition, and daily life – which comprise the daily disciplines required to be fully self-reliant. I am thrilled with the 20-step process in this book and would highly recommend the Harada Method to any organization looking to develop their people to the fullest.

— Susan Howard, Vice President of Talent & Culture, Superior Plastic Products, Key Link Fencing & Railing and Artifex Designs, LLC.

It's been more than 10 years since I travelled to Portland to meet Norman Bodek and attend his Harada Method Certification workshop. I was asked at the end of the course for my overall impression and wrote "Game changing methodology". I still believe that, whether it be for an individual, an enterprise, or indeed a nation. I have been using the Harada Method since then, as well as teaching and coaching others. Apart from the achievement of goals that reflect the best of individual capability, and the real happiness and excitement that comes with that, other impacts I have seen include:

- *Bringing focus and structure to minds and actions that previously reflected chaos and confusion.*
- *Individuals that know daily what needs to be done next, to achieve their goal(s), rather than only reacting to today's issues.*
- *The development of new habits and behaviors through the power of reflection.*
- *The alignment of people within a business with a common goal and the synergy and success that results.*

"The Harada Method starts with establishing a strong goal(s) and an underpinning purpose (the Where), it explores self-awareness and self-reliance (the Now). Most importantly though I believe its value lies in providing the step by step (the How) to

that, I encourage you to add your intention and energy, and with the Harada Method reach for your full potential."
— Brenton Leitch, Managing Director, Learning and Productivity, Australia

"I am excited to start using the tools with such a powerful philosophy behind them."
— John Harding, Lean Manufacturing Manager, LMI Aerospace Inc.

"Thank you so much for introducing me to Harada's method. Harada's work identifies those powerful principles of Self-Reliance and success but puts it into a method that everyone can understand and apply. I see Harada's method as a powerful and necessary cornerstone of success when coupled with the principles of lean manufacturing, vision, and genuine love for other people. For me it closes a long needed gap of work, family, life, and success. I look forward to being a part of this as it sweeps the world in change, as I'm sure it will."
— Bill Wootton, Plant Manager, US Synthetic, winner of the Shingo Prize

"Norman's approach to teaching the method and his amazing experience provided great value to me. The Harada Method provides the means for anyone to establish and reach their goals through a systematic approach that everyone can follow. This method allows the individual to take responsibility for defining their own plan in achieving self-reliance, which will ultimately lead to the accomplishment of higher levels of personal and professional performance."
— Trace P. Tandy, Vice President of Manufacturing, Milbank Manufacturing

"The Harada Method has helped me build the behaviors and routines I needed to be successful in achieving both my work and life goals. I now reflect on my actions and assess their impact against my

goals on a daily basis. This intentional reflection has helped me to improve and has created a level of personal momentum and synergy between my life and my work that I have never experienced."

— Lori Eberhardt, Performance Improvement Advisor, Talisman Energy

"I can see why Harada is considered the best "day-to-day management." I don't know how I've managed to organize myself to date without a comprehensive approach as this."

— Peter Bodi, President, Accurate Machine & Tool Ltd.

"My experience with you was so great. As a lean practitioner, we strive for continuous improvement everyday in our business and client's businesses. The Harada Method is the missing link between continuous improvement, yourself and your mentees. Its comprehensive system allows oneself to take an honest assessment of their life and strive for excellence as well as fulfillment of dreams. Norman's approach is accessible and well suited to individuals of all learning styles. Thank you Norman … for the wonderful experience that has forever changed my approach to developing myself and truly defined my purpose in life."

— Ryan Allen, Total Systems Development

"Norm Bodek has been at the forefront of the business performance improvement movement for more than 30 years. He initially focused on productivity and quality improvement. He was one of the first practitioners to study what was happening in Japan in the early 1980s and has continued to be at the leading edge of finding practical approaches to improve performance.

His newest book, "The Harada Method" is the next step in Norm's on-going learning about finding more effective ways to improve. Takashi Harada developed an effective approach for helping people to become more self-reliant and more successful in their lives. Much of his theory is based on sound research that elite athletes have used for many years: visioning success, specific interim measurable goals, and challenging oneself to be a a better person. This book pulls it all together, in one place. It can supplement the workshops Norm does on this subject; it could also be used by two-or-three people who work together to reinforce what they individually seek to accomplish. This book fits very well with the people side of lean. It would also be a great book for educational institutions to use in working with poor and disadvantaged students as this is where Takashi Harada did his original research and developed his theorie. He was able to help students transform their abilities moving from a life of failure to a life of possibilities, an impressive accomplishment to say the least.

— Michael Bremer, The Cumberland Group

Table of Contents

The Harada Method - the Spirit of Self-Reliance i
Acknowledgments v
Testimonials vii
Introduction xxi
Chapter 1 - Finding Harada 1
  The World's Best Concept on Day-to-Day Management 5
  Meeting Mr. Harada 6
  Three Years Later, the School Became Number One in Osaka 9
  In Harada's own words… 10
    Teaching the Students to be Self-Reliant 11
Chapter 2 – What is the Harada Method? 15
  How is it Done? 16
  Harada Method Overview 16
  Breaking Down the Harada Method Step-by-Step 18
    Step 1 - Believe in Yourself 19
    Step 2 - Become Self-Reliant 19
    Step 4 - The Long-Term Goal Setting - Select Your Main Goal 20
    Step 5 - Setting Different Goal Levels 20
    Step 6 - Set Milestone Goals 21
    Step 7 - State Your Purposes and Values 21
    Step 8 - Analyze Yourself 21
    Step 9 - Create Your 64-Chart with Eight Areas to Achieve Your Goal 22
    Step 10 - Write Eight Tasks for Each Area 22
    Step 11 - Write a Start Date for Each Task 23
    Step 12 - Select 10 Tasks to Get Started 23
    Step 13 - New Routines Build New Habits 23
    Step 14 - Write Affirmations (Self-talk) 24
    Step 15 - Determine the Kind of Support You Need 24
    Step 16 - Select People to Support You 24

Step 17 - Use Your Routine Check Sheet 25
Step 18 - Keep a Daily Diary 25
Step 19 - Work with a Coach/Mentor 25
Step 20 - Revise Your Forms Monthly 25
Everyone can be Successful 26
Become an Astronaut 26
The Harada Method Guides You 30
To Help You Know What You Want Out of Life, We Start by Defining Success: 33
Create a Vision for Yourself 33
Imagine Yourself Being the Best at Something 34
Self-Reliance Means Much More 41
Shaking Up the Financial World 41
The Harada Method Aims to Build Strong Character and Enhance Professional Skills at the Same Time. 44
Enhance Your Spirit, Skills and Physical Condition 45
Something Should be Added: a Daily Life 47
How Can You Become More Self-Reliant? 51
Why is Serving Others Important? 52
When You Serve Others Well, You Break Own Your Own Limitations 53

Case Study - Improving Sales at an Insurance Company 59

Chapter 4 – Select Your Main Goal – The Long-Term Goal Setting Form 63
Section: Top Line 63
Section: Service to Others 64
Goal Setting 65
Know Clearly Why You Want to Achieve Your Goal 65
Take Advantage of Your Education and Prepare Yourself to Succeed in a Tough Job Market 67
Don't Wait for Your Manager to Give You the Opportunity to Grow 70
Harada Value Management: Plan, Think, Write 71
Every Successful Person Has a Script for Their Own Success 72
Add Meaning to Your Job 72
Two Keys to Setting Your Goal: 73
   First Key: Is the Goal Valuable and Worthwhile for You? 73

Second Key: Is the Goal Measurable and Quantifiable Enough that You Will Be Able to Use the Measures to Guide Your Successful Efforts? 73

Chapter 5 - Select Your Goals to Monitor Your Performance 77
Setting Different Goal Levels - The Milestone Goals 78
Highest Goal..................78
Confident or Easiest Goal 79
Intermediate Goal or Moderate Goal 80
Current Capability 80
Use the Goal Types to Understand Your Capabilities..............81
Another Example of Goal Levels 83
Determination Plus Character Make You Successful 85

Chapter 6 - Set Milestone Goals 87
Set Your Goals in Process 87

Case Study - Cosmo Securities Co., Ltd. 89

Chapter 7- State Your Purposes and Values..................91
Purposes Push You Toward Your Goals..................91
Principal Goals Come After Purposes..................91
Intrinsic Goals 92
Tangible: 94
Intangible:..................94
What is Your Purpose in Life? 95
Harada Speaking about Purpose..................96

Chapter 8 - Analyze Yourself 101
Analyzing Successes and Failures..................101
Attributes of Successful People 102
Learn from Your Past Using the Four Aspects 102
Look at Your Past Successes 103
Then Analyze Your Past Failures 105
Why Did You Succeed or Fail? 105
A Few Examples of Past Successes and Failures 106
Predict Future Obstacles and Come up with Solutions..................106
Looking at Problems and Solutions..................107

Chapter 9 - Create Your Open Window 64-Chart with Eight Areas to Achieve Your Goals 109

Case Study - Alpha Studio, Inc. 113

Chapter 10 - Write Eight Tasks for Each Area 115

Chapter 11 - Write a Start Date for Each Task 119
    Add Due Dates 119

Chapter 12 - Select 10 Tasks to Get Started 121

Chapter 13 - Build New Habits With New Routines 123
    How to Pick Your Routines 124

Case Study - J Com 127

Chapter 14 - Write Affirmations (Self-Talk) 131
    Use Sayings to Encourage Yourself and Others 133

Chapter 15 - Determine What Kind of Support You Need .. 135
    Clarify the Support You Need 136

Case Study - ANA Communications Co., Ltd. 137

Chapter 16 - Select People to Support You 139
    Harada's Experience on Becoming a Coach 140

Chapter 17 - Use Your Routine Check Sheet 143
    Breaking Away from Old Ideas 145
    Benefits of the Harada Routine Check Sheet 146

Chapter 18 - Keep a Daily Diary 149
    Use the Power of Writing 155
    The Diary as a Tool for Self-Coaching 156
    The Powerful Impact of the Harada Diary 157
    Managing Your Time Schedule 158
    Praise and Today's Phrase 159
    Challenges and Good Things You Noticed Today 160
    What Would You Do Differently? 160
    Inspiring Words, Phrases, Events 161

Case Study - Sumitomo Life Insurance Company 163

Chapter 19 - Work with a Coach/Mentor 171
　Time Doesn't Flow from the Past to the Future 173
　Tips for coaching 175

Chapter 20 - Revise the Monthly Long-Term Goal Setting Form 179

Chapter 21 - Teams, Self-Reliance and Developing People 181

Case Study - Chugai Pharmaceuticals 185

Chapter 22 - The People Side of Lean - Looking into the Future and Creating an Ideal Workplace 191
　Skill Charts 193

Chapter 23 - Become a Master 195
　Artisans to Artisans - Coming Full Circle 198
　Repetitive Work Does Not Have to Be Bad 199
　Monozukuri and Hitozukuri 200
　Every Employee is Capable of Innovation 203
　Why Training is Important 204

Case Study - A Store Manager at Watami 207

Chapter 24 - Questions from a Certified Student 211

Chapter 25 - An Interview with Jeffrey Liker, Author of *The Toyota Way* 215

Chapter 26 - Interview with Robert Miller, Executive Director of the Shingo Prize 245

Chapter 27 - Interview with John Allen, President, Total Systems Development 259

Chapter 28 - Leadership and Lean: Fifteen Questions for Your Lean Journey 273

Chapter 29 - If You Want to Be Lean, You Need Lean Leaders 277
　Quality of Leaders 277
　Leaders Change Themselves First 277
　"Watch My Tail" 278

Chapter 30 The Difference Between a Leader and an (Old-Thinking) Manager 281
Leadership Versus Management 283

Appendix 1 287
Spotlight – Five Ways to Build Your Mind 287
1. Use Your Mind - Think and Write 287
2. Clean Your Mind - Develop a Feeling of Gratitude 289
3. Strengthening Your Heart 289
"If I Have One Enemy it is Surely my Ego." 290
4. Organizing Your Heart 291
5. Expand Your Heart 293
An Individual Skill Becomes a Corporate Skill, Which Leads the Company to be More Effective. 294
Change 295

Appendix 2 299
PCDSS - A Five-Step Management Cycle for Success 299
Plan - Think and Write 300
Check - Monitor Your Attitude Daily 301
Do - Work Consistently 301
See - Control Yourself and Marshal Your Thoughts 301
Share - Help Others by Sharing Your Ideas and Experiences 302
PCDSS Improves the Whole You 302
Enhance Four Aspects of the "Self" to Gain Valuable Confidence 302

Appendix 3 305
Six Features of a Self-Reliant Person: 305
1. Self-Reliant People are Open-Minded about Advice or Criticism 305
2. Self-Reliant People Take Responsibility for Achieving Their Goals 307
3. Self-Reliant People Believe They Can Win 309
4. Self-Reliant People Create Good Habits 310
5. Self-Reliant People are Reflective Thinkers 311
6. Self-Reliant People Live in Harmony with the Four Aspects: Spirit, Skill, Physical Condition and a Daily Life 313

SUMMARY 315
   The Purposes of the Harada Method 316
   The Harada Method Steps are: 318

INDEX 319

Author Biographies 323
   Norman Bodek 323
   Takashi Harada 331

Introduction

"If you are digging for oil, you must be sure that there is oil under the place you are digging." - Rudi

"The reasons why people cannot achieve their goals are not because they lack abilities or characters, but because they are setting their goals in a wrong way and trying to achieve them in a wrong way."
— Takashi Harada

    A few years ago, I was introduced to "Day-to-Day Management," a methodology created by Takashi Harada. It was claimed to be the world's best process to develop people to their fullest capability. At first, I was both skeptical and fascinated, but I allowed my curiosity to guide me to discover more about the truth. After meeting, Mr. Harada several times, taking a number of his courses in Japan, reading hundreds of translated pages about his work, teaching this methodology to my students at Portland State University, and training and certifying managers, executives and consultants; I am thoroughly convinced of the authenticity of Mr. Harada's work. I hope as you read this book you will agree that his technique is a "jewel" and ranks with the work of Deming, Ohno, Shingo, and other giants of management.

    The Harada Method is a "Sport's Analogy" on how you can take the best from athletics and apply it successfully to your life both on and off the job. I believe we all "love a winner;" but most of us have not been taught how to become one. Here in this book, we give you the steps to carefully follow to transform yourself to a new and very exciting life.

Please note as you read the shaded areas are words directly from Mr. Harada while the un-shaded areas are both my stories and experiences in teaching and using the method.

Over 30 years ago, in 1979, I started a company called Productivity, Inc. in Stamford, Connecticut. At the time American productivity growth rates were declining and the Japanese were advancing at 9% per year. The difference between the two countries was attributed to the Japanese manufacturer's ability to produce and deliver products at low costs with very high quality. My goal at that time was to discover the innovative ideas that the Japanese manufacturers were doing, that we not doing in America, and introduce them to the West. The funny thing is, I wasn't a manufacturing professional. I had never worked a day of my life in a plant – not on the line and not in an office. Yet, I became fascinated with the idea of exploring what was happening in Japan and looking at the possibility of U.S. manufacturers replicating the Japanese methods into their facilities. Remember, this is long before anyone had heard the words Lean, TPM[1], JIT[2], SMED[3], QCC[4], Kaizen Blitz[5] or any of the acronyms so common to most of us today.

---

[1] TPM – Total Productive Maintenance
[2] JIT – Just-in-Time
[3] SMED – Single Minute Exchange of Die
[4] QCC – Quality Control Circles
[5] Kaizen Blitz – a team workshop that radically changes the factory floor

For anyone who knows me, they know that once I get excited about an idea it's hard to hold me back. Nothing as minor as no manufacturing experience and no contacts in Japan was going to stop me. I became interested in looking at the question of why the U.S. productivity rates were dropping while the Japanese rates had increased by 9% that year. I first studied at the library but couldn't find the answer at all and then I went into New York City to attend an "Industry Week" conference and heard a presentation by Joji Arai, manager of Japan Productivity Center's Washington, DC office. After his talk, I went up to him to ask him if he could help me arrange a study mission to Japan. I wanted to get inside some of the world's best plants to see for myself what they were doing. He agreed, and soon I was in Japan walking through Toyota, Canon and other world-class plants. I was hooked. The innovations I saw were breathtaking, and I knew that U.S. manufacturers needed to learn what I was learning.

The next thing you should know about me is that I have an incredible ability to meet some of the world's most amazing people. Maybe it is that I have no fear of picking up the phone and calling someone, (and yes, I have had the phone hung up on me many times), but over the years I have been honored to meet some incredible people – true geniuses. This was definitely true over 30 years ago when I arrived in Japan. On my first few trips, I soon found myself shaking hands with such visionaries as Taiichi Ohno[6], Dr. Shigeo Shingo[7],

---

[6] Taiichi Ohno was the vice president of production for Toyota and the key discoverer of the Toyota Production System.

Dr. Yoji Akao[8] and Dr. Ryuji Fukuda[9] to name a few. These were the people developing what we all know of today as Lean manufacturing. Somehow I managed to have them agree to let me translate their books into English and publish them in America.

Since those early days, I have been to Japan over 80 times, led over 25 study missions, toured more than 250 plants, published over 250 books, ran close to a thousand conferences and seminars and was even inducted into the Industry Week's Manufacturing Hall of Fame. Yet, with all I did to help promote Lean manufacturing, I always felt that something was missing. There was a link that I didn't know about that would pull it all together.

I feel as if I have finally found that link when I learned about Takashi Harada and the Harada Method. Here finally was the next step in the Lean journey. Here was the human side of Lean using a systematic way to develop employees to increase their skill levels to the point that they will become totally self-reliant and virtually

---

[7] Dr. Shigeo Shingo was an independent consultant to Toyota and taught over 3000 of their engineers and managers the principles of Industrial Engineering, problem-solving techniques and the keys to the Toyota Production System. He invented the SMED system and Poka-Yoke.

[8] Dr. Yoji Akao introduced us to Hoshin Planning and QFD.

[9] Dr. Ryuji Fukuda was the vice president of production for Sumitomo Metals, authored my first book Managerial Engineering and introduced me to many of the Lean tools and techniques.

irreplaceable. Yes, Lean has taught us how to continuously make improvements on the shop floor, and now even in our hospitals and other institutions, but what was missing was the way to harness the creativity and motivation of all of our employees and even ourselves. The Harada Method is a personal journey of growth that you can set and achieve your life goals, help lead your employees toward reaching their individual goals and help your organization reach a greater success. It is designed to teach you how to be a great leader, a great coach to develop people to their fullest and to build a winning team.

A few years back, A Chinese fortune cookie told me, "You have the talent to discover the talent in others." Yes, that is my little magic in life to be able to travel the world and to continue to discover true geniuses in management and have the opportunity to bring these discoveries back to American shores. In this book, you will meet Mr. Harada and hear in his own words how he developed his method and what it had meant for countless children and adults throughout Japan. Just as I felt all those years ago when I met Mr. Ohno, Dr. Shingo and the other Lean leaders, I feel the same way now. The Harada Method is life changing. It has changed my life and if you follow me on this step-by-step journey, I am sure that it will change your life too.

In this book, it is our intention to give you a deep understanding of the world's best management training method to teach you how to have a very successful life. It was my miracle to have discovered Takashi Harada, and I now have the privilege to teach his work and to co-author this book. There are many "success" teachers in the world who have written best selling books: Stephen

R. Covey, Malcolm Gladwell, Jack Caldwell, and others, but in my opinion only Takashi Harada really gives you a step-by-step exact method to follow to reach your goals and your personal success. This book is about that method. If you follow the Harada Method you will find your personal and professional success. Let's get started now, looking at what the Harada Method is and how you and your employees can get started learning the steps right away.

Chapter 1 - Finding Harada

"When people pick strong goals, with purposes and values that serve not only themselves but also serve others, their entire character changes."
- Takashi Harada

Selling my business, Productivity, Inc., in 1999, I found myself with time to do some things I always wanted to do but retiring was not one of them. Instead I started to consult, write books, keynote conferences and teach some courses at Portland State University. After taking one of my classes, a group of my students asked if they could intern with me to study Lean principles. The students heard me give a guest lecture on the Best of Japanese Management and they wanted to learn more. We agreed to meet at my office on Friday afternoons, first to discuss ideas and then to learn from Mr. Shigehiro Nakamura over Skype from Tokyo. Mr. Nakamura is a former senior manager with Hitachi Metals and now is an instructor with the Japan Management Association (JMA). He also was the author of The New Standardization: keystone of continuous improvement in manufacturing. Mr. Nakamura has developed over 30 different courses to teach the best of Japanese management.

Every other week, at 8:00am Tokyo time around 4:00pm our time, Mr. Nakamura would review with us his Production Technology MAP, which showed in detail how a company could discover specific steps to take to become world-class competitive.

The MAP is an instrument that gathers the best ideas from a wide group of managers on how to become world-class manufacturers onto one piece of paper. To do this, researchers and consultants of the JMA **studied and benchmarked the best companies in the world** in order to determine what those companies had done to attain their level of superiority. The MAP showed managers and executives what world-class techniques or countermeasures[10] are being used by the world's most successful companies. They wanted not only the entire plant to be world-class but also every part of the operation to be world-class. In the MAP, 38 categories were investigated, including: Quality, Cost, Delivery, Production, Safety/Ecology, Morale, Management Indicators, Standard Manpower, Reviews in Advance, Set-up Improvement, Equipment Management, Automation, Zero-Defect Production, etc.[11]

---

[10] Examples of world-class techniques from the chart: six sigma, zero defect production, productivity of 2 million yen per person, zero injuries, 3 improvement ideas per month per employee, day-to-day-management by objectives, problem potential analysis, design review, SMED, zero failure production, low cost automation, TPM, skill Olympics, design-in, JIT, bipolarization, SAP, hardware Poka-yoke, 3-gen concept, etc.

[11]Technology Transfer, First-Class Skills, Connection Improvement, Target Time Improvement, Hazard Countermeasures, Defect Countermeasures, IE-5S Improvement, Autonomous Maintenance, Workplace Task Forces, Supplier Supports, Total Participation Improvement, Workplace Management Technology, JIT-SCM, Movement Management, IT Online Management, Various Visualizations, Attached Information Management, Materialization of Model Lines, On-site

[Production Technology MAP diagram]

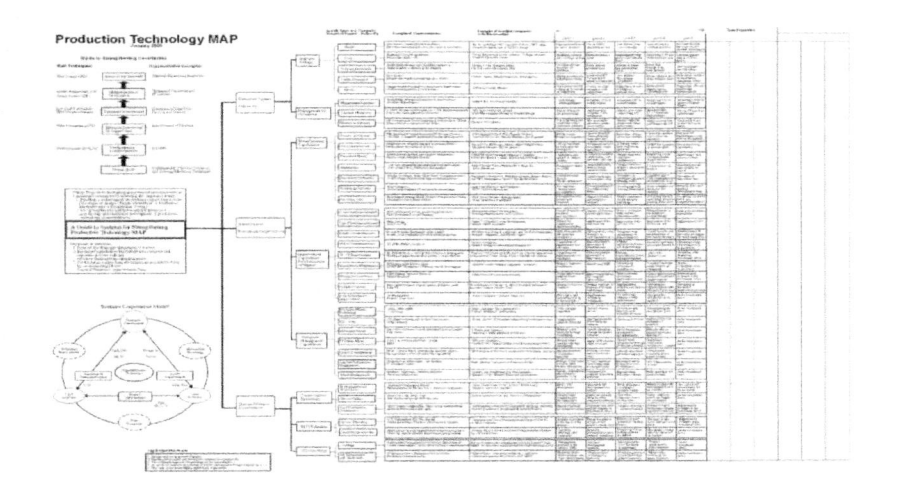

(For a larger, clearer copy of the MAP and/or the forms of the Harada Method, email us at info@pcspress.com).

Within each category on the MAP we saw examples of countermeasures or world-class methodologies being used by the most competitive companies in the world. To the right of the countermeasures were those companies in the world that either developed the methodologies or were using them successfully. For example to the right of quality is Six Sigma and in the next column it says General Electric.

The MAP fascinated me. It was a gold mine! For the past thirty years, I have been looking for the best tools, techniques, and methodologies that would help American companies become more competitive, and here on one sheet of paper was what Mr. Nakamura and

---

Studies, Case Presentation Conferences, In-Class Education, Small Group activities, Coaching and Job Enlargement and Multi-skills.

other leading scholars in Japan considered to be the current best management ideas in the world. Many companies in Japan have used this MAP. Having known Mr. Nakamura for over 20 years and having published his books in English, I trusted his endorsement of the MAP. It was obviously a very valuable instrument to help companies be internationally competitive.

Each week the students and I would take one or more of the categories and ask Mr. Nakamura to explain the details to us. He would send us slides (I have slides in Japanese for over 30 of his courses which go in detail on most of the categories listed.) In addition, Mr. Nakamura also sent us videos.

Having translated and published over one hundred books on Japanese management techniques while I was at Productivity Inc./ Press, I was familiar with many of the techniques on the MAP, but not all of them. Shortly after we began our sessions with Mr. Nakamura, he taught us about the seventh category - "Standard Manpower," that included the following countermeasures: "100% standard time achievement rate + 3% improvement per month" and "Day-to-day management by objectives." The benchmark examples were "Old Canon Production System" and "Daily Management System by Takashi Harada."

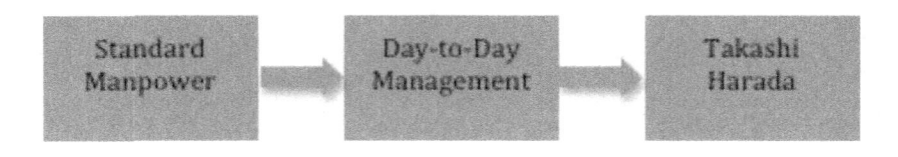

| Standard Manpower | → | Day-to-Day Management | → | Takashi Harada |

The World's Best Concept on Day-to-Day Management

I was somewhat familiar with the Canon Production System[12], but I knew nothing about Takashi Harada and his Daily Management System. Mr. Nakamura gave us some of the details of Mr. Harada's work and sent us a video of Mr. Harada giving a lecture. The video was in Japanese but my wife, Noriko, (who is Japanese), and some of the students, who also knew Japanese, could understand it. They all gave me details about the video. What I heard got me very excited. Most of the categories on the MAP related to process and product improvement, but "day-to-day management" was about how managers could better manage and develop their employees as well as their own careers.

According to the JMA, Takashi Harada's Daily Management System was the **world's best concept on day-to-day management.** It was the best technique for managers to develop their employees and create a new culture within the company. Mr. Harada had found a new way to inspire people to reach for their maximum, creative potential.

The Harada Method compliments the work of Dr. Shigeo Shingo and Taiichi Ohno by addressing the people side of Lean. Virtually every company today is attempting to be Lean, but very few know how to achieve it. The Harada Method can be used to gain full

---

[12] In 1987, at Productivity Inc., I published a book with the title: The Canon Productive System: *Creative Involvement of the Total Workforce*

cooperation for a company's Lean efforts. When people know how to take full responsibility for their own lives and be self-reliant, with the support of management, they can become like an arrow clearly focused on how to be successful personally and also how to better serve well their company. **The Harada Method is the Human Side of Lean.** It overcomes the Eighth Waste of Lean: the underutilization of people's creative talents. It empowers people to take charge of their own life to become highly skilled on the job. It teaches how the company and every employee can be successful at the same time.

Meeting Mr. Harada

My wife Noriko went to Amazon Japan and noted that there were several books written by Mr. Harada. We ordered many of them, and when they came I distributed them to my student interns and Noriko. They were all fascinated reading what Mr. Harada had done and the simplicity and power of the system he had created.

After studying his material, I felt exactly the same way as when I discovered Dr. Shigeo Shingo and Taiichi Ohno. I believed that Japan had another great genius for me to bring to the Western world. I wanted to learn more, so I called Mr. Harada in Osaka. Through Noriko's interpretation, I told him I wanted to come to Japan to meet him, learn more about his methodology and publish his works in English. He agreed to meet me in Tokyo, and I quickly made arrangements to fly to Japan to meet him.

A few weeks later, Noriko and I flew to Japan and met Mr. Harada at a very small hotel in the Asakusa area of Tokyo. In meeting with Mr. Harada, I told him I wanted to take one of his old books and have it translated and published in English, which is what I had done many times when I owned Productivity Inc. Mr. Harada, however, told me he preferred to write a new book for an American audience, and agreed to let me co-author the book, adding in my own understanding of and experiences in teaching his methodology.

Mr. Harada's background is very unique and varied which helped him to develop his method based on his own personal experiences over a number of years. In Japan, Harada is a world-renowned coach, trainer and consultant. But prior to entering the business world, Harada was a junior high school track and field coach at the worst school out of 380 in Osaka, Japan. The school was probably in the most depressed area of Osaka with very few students able to believe that they were capable of achieving anything in their life. Not only were so many of the students failing academically, but few had ever experienced any kind of success athletically. Harada set out to change that and within three years his school became one of the best for athletics and many of the students started to make dramatic improvements academically too. The school became number one in track and field out of hundreds of schools and continued to be number one for the next 6 years in a row - with 13 students winning gold medals and being recognized as the best athletes in their age group in all of Japan. Many of these former underachievers also received scholarships and went on to high school, college and into successful careers in industry.

In 2002, Harada left the school system and opened a consulting practice in Tokyo to teach his method to industry. Since then, he has taught over

55,000 people at 280 companies. Harada first developed his method to transform his underachieving students to turn them into outstanding athletes but soon recognized that he had a powerful method that could help businesses transform their employees too.

Today in Japan, thousands of people who use the Harada Method are improving their lives and contributing more to their companies' bottom lines. They are increasing sales, more successfully implementing projects and working together to set and attain common goals. The Harada Method leads people through a carefully thought-out process, similar to a winning sports team, to build a great company with outstanding employees.

Before starting his consulting business, Takashi Harada, working in one of the poorest neighborhoods in Osaka, was challenged to find a way to help his students become winners - to have personal success in addition to being outstanding athletes. He felt his students were underachievers. Many of those students did not want to come to school; very few went to high school and almost none went on to college. Mr. Harada, however, felt that he could bring positive change and motivate the students to become better athletes.

Mr. Harada noticed that there were schools in Osaka that were consistently successful in track and field. He thought, "If another coach in Osaka can produce a winning team, so can I! The other coaches have to get athletes from their local areas too." **Harada realized that he could not just pick winners; he had to somehow develop them.**

It was not at all easy and he faced a lot of resistance. For example, one day, students and parents, with the school principal in attendance, confronted Mr. Harada. "You are too hard on our children," they said. Mr. Harada replied, "I want your children to be winners. Do you want your children to be winners or do you want them to stay where they are? If you give me three years, I will make this the best school in the city in track and field and if I don't, then fire me."

Three Years Later, the School Became Number One in Osaka

Mr. Harada found a method to take those underprivileged children and make them winners. To the students, winning the competition felt like winning an Olympic medal. The junior high school also substantially improved academically. As the athletes became winners, their success was noticed by the other students and drove them to improve as well.

How was it possible to take those children who had so few advantages at both their homes and at school, and motivate them to work on themselves to become winners? That is what this book is about. Mr. Harada believes every person can and should be allowed to pick their own success goal, something that will get them excited about their life and futures. Of course, if you work for an organization, you want the goal to be in alignment with those of your company. Virtually anyone can be a master at some discipline given the guidance and willingness to work hard over a period of time and with the perseverance and belief that their goal can be obtained. When you have a personal goal, something to strive after, work takes on a whole new meaning.

In Harada's own words...

When I started teaching at a junior high school, I tried to make most of my strengths of leading and managing people effectively. This was an important part of what I call a "self-managing practice" in the Harada Method—realizing your own strengths and putting it into practice.

All three junior high schools in Osaka where I worked before leaving teaching were difficult schools to teach at. Arguably they were the toughest schools to teach at in all of Osaka. In addition to having difficult students, the parents were also very hard to deal with. In some cases, both parents in a family would be drug addicts who were in jail. In others, fathers acted like gang leaders, threatening me for challenging their children to improve. By far, the worst incident was when a parent killed his child for some unknown reason. These were just a few terrifying things that I experienced while at these tough schools. Still, I voluntarily chose to work at these schools to utilize my strong leadership skills.

At Matsumushi Junior High School, the last school I worked at before becoming a consultant, I found that many students and parents were strikingly different from my two previous schools. Some of the students never stepped inside the classrooms. Bullying was rampant. Many parents were obstacles to their children's learning and growth. Other parents worked long hours, neglecting to spend time with their children.

In the neighborhood near the school, poor workers took out their frustration out on each other and clashed violently with each other. At certain corners of the school zone, buying and selling illegal drugs was a usual occurrence. In addition to living in such a terrible environment, the biggest problem was that students and parents lacked the desire and motivation to live a meaningful life.

Teaching the Students to be Self-Reliant

"After a week or so working in the school, I realized that the majority of the students did not care about their schoolwork because they had no dreams to live for. They had no future vision that helped direct them. Their typical answers for my questions were, "I can't do that because I'm not smart enough," or "That's impossible because I'm not cut out for it."

"Soon, I figured out where their answers came from. Their answers were the same as those of their parents: "My kid can't do that, because she is not smart enough," or "That's impossible for my sons, because they are not cut out for it." No matter how much I tried to convince the parents of their child's great potential as an athlete, they always said disapprovingly, "She will never, ever make it." The students just copied the words that their parents used to deflect other people's positive messages.

"To really find out what both the students had in mind for their futures, I continued to ask them, 'Don't you want to be a gold medalist?' They always replied, "It's impossible. But I would not give up, asking them repeatedly. Don't you really want to be a gold medalist?" Eventually, they would admit, "I would be like to be a gold medalist, if I could."

"I asked their parents the same question, "Don't you want your child to be a champion athlete?" The parents would say that their child had no way to make it. After repeatedly asking the same question, they would finally admit that they really wanted their child to be successful and, if possible, a champion. They would also say, "I wish my child had a better chance to succeed as a student."

"Through conversations with the students and the parents, I learned that both groups actually had dreams, but that they had lost the belief they could make their dreams come true. They saw hundreds of homeless people occupying the street corners of the school zone, a countless number of single-parent households and terrible economic instability that made it hard to continue their education. Because of these problems, students and parents suffered and could not afford to think about the dreams they once had.

"'How can I help them?' I wondered. As a schoolteacher and coach, I wanted to help these people gain control over their lives by pushing them to accomplish something meaningful and therefore gaining confidence in themselves. Even if they did not have enough parental or financial support, I wanted them to understand that they could succeed in life and become better people.

"After much thought, I realized what I was supposed to do for these people. By promoting educational efforts and sports programs, I could help them understand the importance of having dreams and clear goals in life. Having dreams and goals helps guide people in the right direction. It helps them build great character and it eventually helps them succeed in their lives.

"The thing my students needed most was to learn how to be self-reliant. Being self-reliant would help them get on the right track, even without having parents or adults guiding them. Once they learn how to be self-reliant, students can think, decide, and act to make their dreams come true and achieve their goals. From that day forward, I started to promote the idea of self-reliance among students in the school who had been helpless and apathetic. "

After helping thousands of children turn their lives around, Mr. Harada left the school system and started his consulting company in Tokyo to teach his methodology to industry, using the principles that were applied to a winning sports team at his school to now working at hundreds of companies across Japan. Now Harada has countless examples where troubled companies went from loss to profits almost overnight after they started following the Harada Method, just as he had done for the students.

Just a few of the companies Mr. Harada has worked with over the past ten years includes: Cosmo Securities Co., LTD. who used the Harada Method to change its red ink to black. Every employee, including the CEO, was trained. The general managers were able to expand their own capabilities and significantly improve their stores performances. Alpha Studio, Inc. implemented the method and profits improved 200%. Mr. Okuda, a manager at Juniper Telecommunications Co. Ltd took six months to transform his branch office from the lowest performer to number one in the company. Juniper has 9,400 employees in 46 different countries.

By studying the world's best sports coaches and successful teachers, Mr. Harada developed a very powerful and unique process to guide people to be able to fulfill their goals. I have seen it work with almost all of my students at Portland State University and with dozens of managers in American industry. The power of the method and what makes it so unique is that you take over the responsibility for your own success by picking a goal to be successful in your life and following a step-by-step process to attain that goal.

Chapter 2 – What is the Harada Method?

*Champions aren't made in the gyms.
Champions are made from something
they have deep inside them -- a desire,
a dream, a vision. – Muhammad Ali*

The essence of the Harada method is what we call "self-reliance." Self-reliance is the ability of each person to become so skilled at something that she or he is virtually irreplaceable. They become artisans in disciplines they choose that serve their future and also the success of their organization. People are fully trusted to make responsible decisions for themself and for the organization they work for. The Harada Method helps you produce a clear map on how to achieve your goals and how to develop your talents, and the talents of people that work for you, to everyone's fullest potential.

The Harada Method Works for an Individual, a Team of People and for the Total Organization

The purpose of this book is to help you learn how to "take charge of your life," to think about your future and turn what you want into reality. We do not tell you what to pick for your career, nor do we tell you what success means. We want you to be self-reliant and to decide these things for yourself. We only want to give you the proven tools that will provide you with a marvelous life. Of course, you will have to work hard for your success, but at least you will be working towards something that you want to do.

If you are a manager of people, this book will help you become a more effective leader and coach, able to teach people to become self-reliant. The real key is to understand deeply what self-reliance is, what is its value and purpose, and how to apply it in your life and the lives of people that work for and with you. The Harada Method will show you how to become a "winner," by following a step-by-step process for setting and achieving personal and corporate goals.

How is it Done?

Throughout this book we will go into great detail on each step of the method, but here is a brief overview of the different steps and some of the forms that you will be completing as you move through each chapter. Take a quick look at each form, but don't try to get started before we explain Harada's reasons for developing each step and accompanying form.

Harada Method Overview

The Harada Method is a system that provides you a framework for reaching your goals and achieving success. You will see the following five forms as we proceed throughout the course:

1. **33 Questions for Self-Reliance** – gauges how self-reliant you see yourself.

2. **Long-Term Goal Form** – the heart of the Harada Method. This form is the main tool that organizes your goals and purposes, your self-analysis and your action plan.

WHAT IS THE HARADA METHOD? 17

3. **Open Window 64 Chart** – a framework for coming up with the tasks and routines you need to complete to accomplish your goals.

4. **Routine Check Sheet** – a daily checklist to help you strengthen your habits.

5. **Daily Diary** – a planning tool that helps you organize each day to improve your productivity. It also teaches you to reflect on each day so that you can gauge your daily progress.

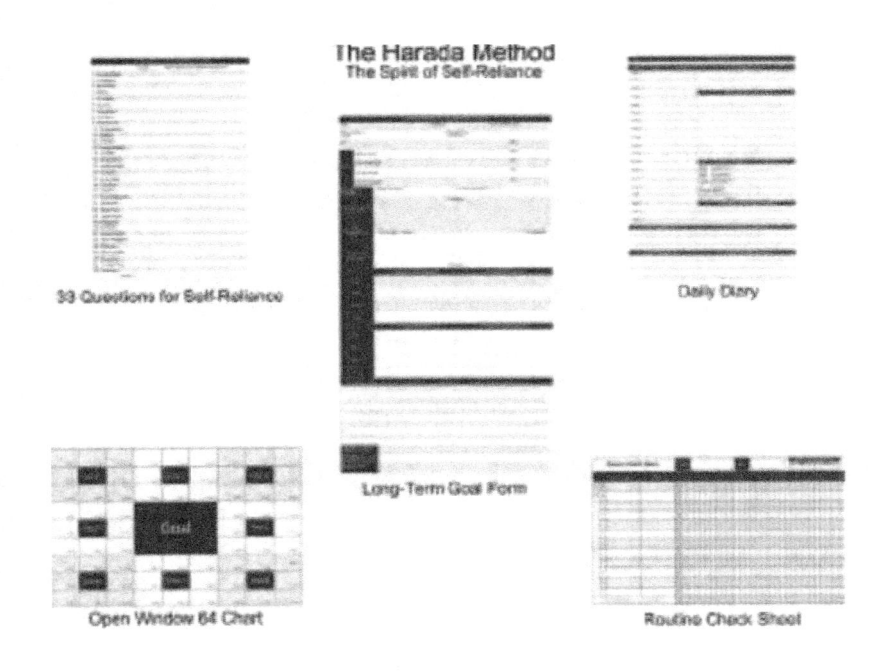

33 Questions for Self-Reliance

The Harada Method
The Spirit of Self-Reliance

Daily Diary

Open Window 64 Chart

Long-Term Goal Form

Routine Check Sheet

To complete each of the five above forms you will first have to follow the five overarching steps of the method, which are:

Goal → Purpose → Analysis → Action → Implement

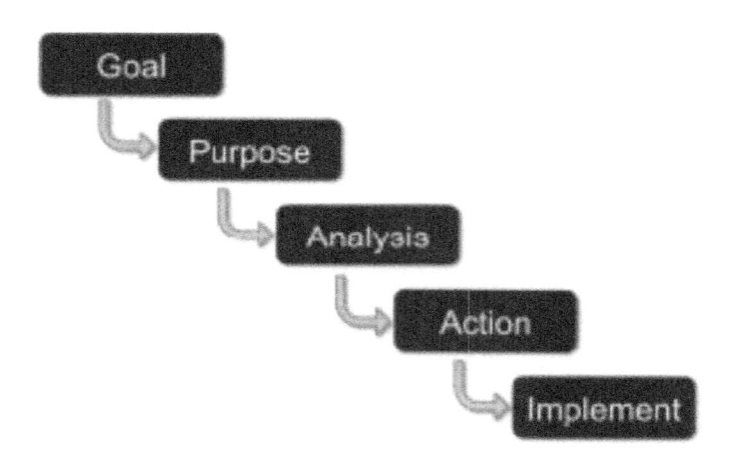

1. **Goal** - picking a goal that is right for you.

2. **Purpose** - understanding why you want to achieve this goal. The stronger your purpose, the easier it will be for you to reach your goal.

3. **Analysis** - looking at the past and potential future to re-enforce your strengths and eliminate your failures.

4. **Action** - building an action plan.

5. **Implement** - incorporating your plan into your daily life, making yourself accountable for your actions, and sustaining your efforts.

Breaking Down the Harada Method Step-by-Step

We can further break down the five main steps into 20 basic steps of the Harada Method. They are not necessarily complicated, but they do require you to put in the effort and to do them diligently. The steps are:

Step 1 - Believe in Yourself

It is vital for you **to believe** that you can and will be successful in both your personal and professional life. Understanding how the Harada Method has worked for others will give you confidence that you can indeed reach your goals.

Step 2 - Become Self-Reliant

As we mentioned before, the Harada Method is based on the idea of self-reliance. Throughout this book you will see the terms self-reliant, self-directed, self-realized, self-determined and autonomous used interchangeably, all meaning having the ability to "stand on your own two feet," - to have the confidence and the skills to reach your personal and professional goals. No matter what is happening in the world around you - an economic recession[13], political turmoil, etc. - you should put your energy into what you can do to improve your life and the lives of others around you. If you can get passionate about something and develop a deep knowledge of a subject, you will become self-reliant-possessing the wisdom to know how to use that skill for the betterment of society and yourself.

---

[13] Price Industries manufactures commercial air-conditioning. The recession has reduced their potential market by 30% but they doubled their sales by 50% in the last three years. They are very good at what they do.

Step 3 - Determine the Key Service to Others

It took me some time to understand Harada's principle of making service to others an important part of attaining success. In America, we come from a culture that fosters the individual to succeed on his or her own. We are "rugged individualists," coming from the Wild West mentality. Sure, we give to charity and are good to our families and friends, but we are taught to be fiercely competitive in the world of business. Being fiercely competitive is fine, but you should also include others in your ambition. Further on in the book, Mr. Harada will show you how serving others is an important key to your own success.

Step 4 - The Long-Term Goal Setting - Select Your Main Goal

To move the process forward, you need to select a goal to be successful in life. You decide what you want to do. It is not easy to pick a goal, but you can do it. When I was young, I studied to be an accountant because my father and brother were accountants. I was not sure what I wanted to do. Fortunately, I found a new goal for my life and left accounting just three years after graduating from college, eventually becoming a publisher, writer, teacher and lecturer – a more fulfilling career for me.

Step 5 - Setting Different Goal Levels

In the Harada Method you will set four kinds of goals: highest goal, intermediate or moderate goal, confident or easiest goal and what you think you can do with your current capability. When you have a series of goals, you are preparing to stretch yourself.

It is not always easy to leap from your current state to attaining your highest goal so we set interim goals. We want to set levels to strive for.

Step 6 - Set Milestone Goals

It would be nice if we could reach all our goals at once, without getting lost in the process of pursuing them. However, we often get frustrated in the middle of pursuing a goal because we cannot see our progress. For some reason, we do not know what is right or wrong when we are in the middle of doing something. To overcome this, write down some measurable milestone goals between the time you start and your goal due date to help motivate you to stay on track.

Step 7 - State Your Purposes and Values

Your goal has value for others and for yourself. The deeper the purpose and the more meaningful it is to you and to others, the easier it will be for you to attain your goal. An example of a purpose: "If I can attain my goal, I know my family will have a better life - my children can go to college. They are depending on me to succeed - so I will."

Step 8 - Analyze Yourself

We want you to repeat behaviors that led you to success in the past. To do this, think of your past successes and write them down. Then write down the reasons you succeeded, using the following categories: mental, skills, health/physical condition and life/living (we will explain the categories in more detail later in the book). Repeat the process for your past failures and challenges, except that this time write the behaviors you want to avoid repeating.

Step 9 - Create Your 64-Chart with Eight Areas to Achieve Your Goal

The 64-Chart is a matrix that helps you determine the tasks and actions you will need to take in the future to achieve your goals. You start by writing your main goal in the center box. Then you write down eight areas that will support your goal. If your goal is to be the "Best Harada Method Teacher," for example, you might write down: Study, Marketing, Public Speaking, Teaching, Writing, etc. for your areas. We'll get into greater detail on this chart in Chapter 9.

Step 10 - Write Eight Tasks for Each Area

After coming up with the eight areas, you then write eight specific tasks within each area. For example, one of the eight areas in the example from Step 9 is "Study," so you would write eight tasks, one in each box around the word Study. Some examples:

"I want to read as much of Harada's material as possible. This means I have to get his books translated into English."

"I want to read books and listen to videos done by great athletic coaches."
"I want to study and review the best training material on the subject."

Step 11 - Write a Start Date for Each Task

Once you have brainstormed 64 tasks, you need to reach your goals. You want to determine which ones to do first. Write down the date when you want to get started with each task. Do this for as many tasks as you can.

Step 12 - Select 10 Tasks to Get Started

Go over your 64-Chart, look at the dates and prioritize the top ten tasks that you want to start doing immediately to attain your goal. Include the date when you want to start and complete each task.

Step 13 - New Routines Build New Habits

On the Long-Term Goal Form, write 10 routines you want to do regularly to create positive habits and behaviors. The 10 routines can come from your 33 Self-reliant words, from your analysis section or from the 64-Chart. These routines will help you to build new patterns and behaviors.

Step 14 - Write Affirmations (Self-talk)

Affirmations are statements that will keep your energy positive as you work towards achieving your goal. For example, this past winter I was watching the New York Knicks playing the Dallas Mavericks and with the outstanding performance of Jeremy Lin the Knicks won. Throughout the game, you could see the shouts of encouragement from one player to another. They huddle and cheer themselves to make them all believe they can win. The team uses certain chants to create the proper mindset for the game. You can do the same thing for yourself by writing affirmations.

Step 15 - Determine the Kind of Support You Need

Think about the kinds of support you need to reach your goal. Will you need information? Advice? Coaching? Will you need someone to help you submit your new plan to your boss? Write down whatever types of support you think you might need to accomplish your goals.

Step 16 - Select People to Support You

No one can be successful on their own. Even Tiger Woods, one of the world's greatest golfers, always worked with a coach to observe his swings and body movements and help him improve his performance. Write down the names of people you can ask for help to reach your goal.

Step 17 - Use Your Routine Check Sheet

Using the Routine Check Sheet every day, keep track of how many routines you did. You take the routines from the Long-Term Goal Setting and write them on the Routine Check Sheet. Here you will record every day your success in keeping your promises to yourself.

Step 18 - Keep a Daily Diary

Use the Daily Diary to schedule your activities and to focus on the tasks and actions that need to be done to work closer to your goals. At the end of each day, use the diary to reflect on the challenges and successes that occurred throughout the day.

Step 19 - Work with a Coach/Mentor

Meet with your coach/mentor as often as possible to review your Daily Diaries.

Step 20 - Revise Your Forms Monthly

At the end of every month, look back at your Long-Term Goal Setting and your Routine Check Sheet and make any necessary revisions. If you have accomplished some of the tasks, replace them with new ones. If you would like to focus on new routines for the month, write them down too.

I know that the above list of steps might seem overwhelming, but don't worry. In future chapters, we go through each step, one at a time, giving you specifics of what you need to do and how. Remember, these steps took Harada many years to develop and he, and thousands of people, has experienced great success following the steps. It's definitely worth the time and effort.

Everyone can be Successful

Harada says, "Everyone can be successful." This is absolutely true, but you have to want it and you have to be willing to work for it. We don't tell you what is success; you decide that for yourself. We do recommend that you pick a goal that is good for you, for society and good for your company at the same time.

Unfortunately, we were rarely ever asked to set future goals while we were going to school. Yes, we had to go to school, and I hated it, and without a goal it was as if I was going to school without any purpose at all. It is like a boat on the ocean bobbling up and down in the waves not knowing where the destination is.

Here's an example of how you could use the Harada Method to set the goal of becoming an astronaut. Although this is not a career goal many can have, it will illustrate how you could use the Harada Method to work towards this lofty goal.

Become an Astronaut

Imagine you want to be an astronaut, a person trained by a human spaceflight program to command, pilot, or serve as a crewmember of a spacecraft. From where you are right now in life, what would you have to do to become an astronaut? The Harada Method helps you create a detailed plan of how to get there, using the following process:

WHAT IS THE HARADA METHOD?

1. **First and most important - you have to believe in yourself and that you are capable of becoming an astronaut.** You drop off any doubt. You know that you have a lot of hard work in front of you, but you are confident and willing to do whatever is necessary to attain your goal.

2. **You evaluate yourself on a scale of one to ten using the 33 self-reliant words.** Then you determine what you will do to move up your capability on those words where you score yourself less than ten.

3. **You clearly define your goal and your vision for the future.** You write down exactly what you want to do as an astronaut and the date when you want to become one (e.g., "By March 2018, I want to be an astronaut studying the relationship between weightlessness and bone density"). Writing down the goal helps you create a clear vision for what you will become in the future.

4. **You develop interim goals** with specific measures and dates to monitor your progress. The interim goals remind you when you have to finish certain key things if you want to reach your overall goal on time (e.g., "I want to finish my Ph.D. in physiology by 2016").

5. **You look deeply within yourself to discover the real purpose and value** of becoming an astronaut and what the tangible and intangible benefits will be for yourself and for others. An example of a tangible benefit for you would be to

"make enough money as an astronaut to pay off my student loans from the Ph.D. program." An intangible benefit might be that you will be "awed by the feeling of seeing Earth from outer space for the first time." "I know that I will be a very happy person as I strive for my goal and when I attain it." Also, you will state the purpose of attaining your goal for others: "The world will become a safer place as countries cooperate to study the value of developing outer space stations." "My family will be very proud of my accomplishments."

6. **You analyze your past successes** to understand why you were successful (e.g., "I was able to ace my entrance exam because I studied constantly during the two months leading up to it."). You look at your past successes to be able to repeat those positive behaviors and habits in the future.

7. **You also analyze your past failures** so you can identify negative behaviors and prevent yourself from repeating them (e.g., "I was passed over for a promotion because instead of putting in extra time at the lab, I left work often to watch baseball").

8. **You anticipate any obstacles that might stand in the way** of your success. If you know what challenges you might face in the future, you will be able to deal with them easier (e.g. "I might not be physically strong enough to handle the demands of the astronaut training").

9. **You write countermeasures to the obstacles** (e.g., "I will join a gym and find a workout partner to keep me accountable for exercising").

10. **You create a list of detailed tasks and actions, using the 64-Chart,** that you will have to do to build your skills and capabilities to become an astronaut. Over time, you work to complete all of the necessary tasks on the chart to attain your goal.

11. **You write a list of routines** that you will do this month to do daily (or almost daily) to build new patterns that keep you on the right path. You develop the routine list to reinforce positive behaviors. The routines can come from: your 33 self-reliant words, an analysis of your past successes or failures or from the tasks on the 64-chart (e.g., "I will work late in the lab two days a week," or "I will spend 30 minutes each day reading the latest medical research on the effects of gravity on the human body"). You want to create new habits or behaviors to continually move closer and closer to your goal even when you are not consciously thinking about it.

12. **You write down the kind of support you will need from others** to attain your goals and also you will indicate the kind of support you might need (e.g., "I will need Dr. Ellsbury to teach me how to set up a bone density monitoring experiment").

13. **You keep a daily diary showing your schedule for each day**. The diary helps you organize your time and to focus on the most important tasks for each day. It also gives you a space for daily reflection so you can prepare better for the next

day. Over time, using the diary ingrains your new habits and incorporates the Harada Method into your daily life.

14. **Lastly you work with a coach/mentor to help you perform the tasks needed to succeed.** Without a coach you might lose your will and allow yourself to fall back to previous habits.

You may not necessarily become an astronaut, but by following the Harada Method, you can reach your goal of obtaining the career of your dreams. The method takes what originally seemed almost impossible and makes it attainable. The stronger you can visualize your goal, the easier it will be for you to accomplish and fulfill your dream.

The Harada Method Guides You

The above steps are a shortened version of the Harada Method - in the book we will review each step in greater detail on your different forms. When you complete each step, fill in the details and proceed to follow them every day, you will give yourself the greatest chance of success. The Harada Method acts as your guide, it does not tell you what to do. When you can pick your own goal, instead of just doing what someone else wants you to do, you can become highly motivated and excited to succeed.

Preparing for a sports competition is similar to working in business. Throwing the javelin, for example, is not easy and takes many hours of practice, but athletes with clear goals are able to go beyond the pain and stay on course. You can do the same at work when you establish clear goals. When you pick your own growth goal and deeply believe in your ability to attain that goal, virtually nothing can prevent you from attaining it. If you decide to run a triathlon six months from now, nothing, except an accident, will stand in the way of your practice! If you decide to become your company's number one salesperson, nothing will stand in your way!

Harada developed his steps and tools after many years of trying different ways to motivate his students. Through trial and error he came up with four areas to focus on: spirit, skill, physical condition and routine. He created four tools which we saw above: Long-Term Goal Setting , 64–Chart, Daily Diary and the Routine Check Sheet to help his students better manage their lives and to help them reach their individual goals.

As Harada explains:

> "Once you obtain this skill of knowing how and where to put your efforts, all you have to do is to repeat it as if you were walking down a familiar street. I went through many hardships to coach my first champion. After that, things began to come easier by **following the principles of success.**[14] I knew exactly what I had to do to accomplish my goals, and I did what I had decided to do. In my last year at Matsumushi, a boy reached #1 in the shot put (he was previously 13th). I did nothing special to make him a champion. His transformation to reach #1 was like an automated process; as if everyone knew from the very beginning that he would be a champion. He just clearly visualized the success of his

---

[14] The Principles of Success are the steps of the Harada Method

goal, developed a plan to attain that goal and then worked on himself, every day, to achieve it.

This is how the process worked. First, I made a strong push to let students in Matsumushi have dreams. I wanted people in the Matsumushi region to know that dreams can come true. I wanted to give them hope and courage. I wanted to raise them up and let them know that they had the potential to achieve even their wildest dreams. I wanted them to believe in themselves."

From years of trial and error, the truth finally came to me. By harmonizing "spirit, skill, physical condition and daily life (the four aspects)," you are enabled to manage your life by yourself. This is what being self-reliant is all about.

Improving the four aspects - spirit, skill, physical condition, and daily life - also applies to adults who are working in society. **What you do when you leave the workplace greatly influences what you can achieve from nine to five at your workplace.** If you have troubles with your wife, it might disturb your concentration at your job. If you stay up late at night doing nothing but watching TV, it can harm your health, resulting in lower work performance. In order to do your best work, you have to be aware of how important all four aspects are.

I personally do not regard success as some kind of miracle. I found many important principles to help people succeed. Among them, the most important is that success is a skill that you can attain through making an effort. Once you obtain this skill of knowing how and where to put your efforts, all you have to do is to repeat it as if you were walking down a familiar street. I went through many hardships to coach my first champion. After that, things began to come easier by **following the principles of success.** I knew exactly what I had to do to accomplish my goals.

To Help You Know What You Want Out of Life, We Start by Defining Success:

1.　List several people you consider to be highly successful:
___
___
___

2.　What qualities do these people have in common?
___
___
___

3.　How do you define success for yourself?
___
___
___

Create a Vision for Yourself

Once you define success, you then create a very strong vision for your future. Harada tells you to look into the future and picture yourself being successful. Then all you have to do is work backwards by reviewing the steps you took to get there.

Imagine Yourself Being the Best at Something

You can use the Harada Method to attain both short- and long-term goals. To learn the process, you might like to pick a goal to complete this month, but to me the Harada method is most powerful in picking a long-term meaningful goal.

You want to strive to be great, to be the best in the world at something. This is my goal:

> **"I want to be the best teacher teaching managers how to teach their employees how to be successful in life. I also want to be the best teacher teaching teachers how to teach their students how to be successful in life."**

It is a tall order for me, but it gives me something to shoot for the rest of my life. Some days it seems like this mountain - my ambition - is too hard to climb. To keep going, I just use Harada's motto, "Never Give Up." I pick myself up every day and continue to do my absolute best to attain my goals.

Ask your employees what their favorite day of the week is. I do this often when I speak to groups. Almost everyone loves Friday or Saturday. Why? Why isn't Monday the best day of the week? It can be, if you take charge of your life and pick goals that get you excited at both work and home. I believe you can make work fun. You can even do the exact same job as you do now, but your whole spirit will change when you can see new opportunities in the future for you.

Harada says **"work is life,"** and we should all make life a joyous experience. It might not be easy, but work should be fulfilling and it should be a pleasure to get up and go to work. As you will see as you learn the Harada Method, you can make work a thrilling experience. I am not against retirement but I don't know if I will ever be ready for it. I am too excited at this moment teaching the Harada Method.

Most of my students never before really picked a concrete goal. They wanted to find a good job after graduation and were hopeful that the new company would offer them something interesting to do while they work. The students are happy to get a job but often are not fulfilled when someone else sets the goal for them.

Many people that I have met in industry also have no concrete goals. They go to work, do their job but can't wait for Saturday to come around. At a recent Lean conference in Winnipeg, Canada, I asked 60 people in my workshop, "Who has a definite goal that will lead you to be successful in life?" Five hands went up. Then I asked them to tell me what their goals were and two immediately said their goal was to retire.

Now that you have seen an overview of the Harada Method, it's time to start learning more of the specific details of the method so you can start working towards setting and achieving your goals today.

Chapter 3 - Become Self-Reliant

> "Winning means you're willing to go longer, work harder, and give more than anyone else." - Vince Lombardi, former football coach, Green Bay Packers

As we mentioned earlier, self-reliance is the heart of the Harada Method. It is the recognition that you have the intelligence and the ability to make the best decisions for your organization, your customers and everyone else involved. It means that you can be fully trusted to make those right decisions without close monitoring by your superiors. Self-reliance primarily comes from developing your knowledge, your skills, your character and allowing your deep wisdom to shine through you. When someone is self-reliant, they are successful, reliable, trustworthy, highly skilled and able to make the best decisions for themselves, their family, their associates and for the organization they work for.

We normally consider senior managers to be fully self-reliant, trusted to make the correct decisions for the company. However, this level of trust does not exist at all levels of most companies. When people are not viewed as self-reliant, they are closely monitored and restricted in what they do. The Harada Method eliminates the need to constantly monitor lower-level employees...saving a great deal of time and money. By using the Harada Method, each person in an organization can become self-reliant, so they can be trusted to make the right decisions for the company and for themselves.

From a company's perspective, self-reliance means that workers can be more and more respected and trusted to make the good choices on the job, especially when they interact with customers. When employees are not fully self-reliant, companies closely monitor them to ensure they make the right decisions. Front line people are given scripts to read, are "monitored for quality purposes," have long lists of rules to follow and often are limited in how they are allowed to relate to their customers.

How often when you call a company do you get the message? "We are recording this conversation for quality purposes." Do you know of any company that monitors calls to senior management, rarely if at all?

If you were a Boy or Girl Scout, you might remember the Scout's Law.[15] Isn't this exactly what we want of our self and others at work?

We don't trust the front line people because we do not educate them properly. We do not develop a learning and growth path for them. The solution goes back to self-

---

[15] *A Boy Scout is: Trustworthy, Loyal, Helpful, Friendly, Courteous, Kind, Obedient, Cheerful, Thrifty, Brave, Clean, and Reverent.*

"I will do my best to be honest and fair, friendly and helpful, considerate and caring, courageous and strong, and responsible for what I say and do, and to respect myself and others, respect authority, use resources wisely, make the world a better place, and be a sister to every Girl Scout."

reliance, passing more and more responsibility to the workers to be highly skilled and able to detect and prevent problems. A self-reliant person can be confident to handle different situations and challenges that come their way. Can you really work for someone else and be self-reliant? Of course you can.

UniQlo

UniQlo is one of the fastest-growing clothing store chains in the world where you can buy well-made, fashionable clothing at very reasonable prices. The stores are filled with merchandise up to the ceiling, all perfectly arranged, neatly folded and properly displayed. I like to visit the store that is located on the Ginza in Tokyo, whenever I go to Japan.

Mr. Harada told me this story about the company, which he said underscores the importance of all employees being self-reliant.

A woman carrying a baby came into a UniQlo store and asked to use the store phone to call a doctor for her child, who was very sick. The clerk was very apologetic but told the woman that the company's policy manual forbids the use of company telephones by customers. He did not let the customer use the telephone.

In desperation, the woman went next door with her sick child and was able to call an ambulance. A few days later, she wrote a letter to Tadashi Yanai, the president of UniQlo, to express her anger and frustration. Feeling personally ashamed by the incident, Mr. Yanai, reported to be the richest man in Japan, called Mr. Harada requesting that he teach Uniglo employees self-reliance.

Now, after the Harada Method training, Mr. Yanai's employees have learned to balance the needs of customers with the needs of the company, and they have a sense of pride and accomplishment when they do the right thing, even if it might slightly go against company policy.

Toyota also teaches their workers to be self-reliant. The company has a system called Jidoka[16] where every person has the power to stop the line. A worker can pull a red cord and cause a hundred people to stop work. Toyota wants to prevent every defect from moving along the line. When the cord is pulled, the supervisor and fellow workers run over to help, and the line stops for only seconds - but it can happen 50 times a day. A new worker learns very quickly to become self-reliant – feeling comfortable stopping the line when necessary. Instead of recording for quality purposes, this same technique can

---

[16] Jidoka - Japanese word meaning "automation with a human touch."

be applied in the call centers - fellow workers can help each other when new employees run into difficulties.[17]

Self-Reliance Means Much More

When people focus on building their own success while serving others at the same time, they fulfill the real definition of self-reliance. It is like being a Boy Scout or Girl Scout. There is a certain honor you receive when you are growing personally and also serving others at the same time.

To be self-reliant, you must be a person of high character with good skills and knowledge about your job and your responsibilities. Self-reliance also means that you are a person with integrity and confidence who knows how to live up to your commitments.

Shaking Up the Financial World

In the fall of 2008, after Lehman Brothers collapsed and the sub-prime loan crisis was in full swing, the world economy became increasingly chaotic. The Japanese economy fell into disarray and even major Japanese multi-national companies, which have strong overseas operations and are usually immune from economic downturns, also suffered greatly. Japanese

---

[17] At the end of every day, workers in small teams review all of the problems faced during the day and ask each other questions: "What can we do to not repeat the problems?" "What can we do to give better customer service?" What can we do to be more self-reliant?" You will be amazed at the positive change that will take place.

Prime Minister Aso called it 'an unprecedented economic crisis.'

The damage to the Japanese economy was obvious. Japanese companies were under great pressure to reduce the size of their workforce, and they laid people off very quickly, particularly temporary workers. The rise in unemployment pushed many people out of their homes, and large numbers of homeless people could be seen milling around the parks in downtown Tokyo. During the New Year holidays, when workers traditionally take a longer break to celebrate with their families, hundreds of thousands of unemployed workers were not able to find overnight shelter, let alone jobs.

The year 2008 happened to be a very significant year for me as well. In July, just before the market collapse, I started my new company, the Harada Education Institute, moving my office from Tokyo to Osaka. Osaka, the second largest city in Japan (and my hometown), has an economy based around the securities industry as well as the retail and manufacturing sectors.

The recession deeply affected my new business. Due to the crisis, many of my clients cut back their budgets and had to revisit their contracts with me. I clearly remember one day in late September 2008, when a manager from a major Japanese bank flew into Osaka from Tokyo for an urgent meeting. His bank had already introduced my human resource development program, the Harada Method for Self-Reliance, to its employees. The bank also contracted with my firm to provide training for its executives.

The bank representative arrived in my office with a rather panicked expression on his face. He apologetically broke the bad news that he had no choice but to cancel our contract for employee training because of the bank's deep financial troubles.

"The firm told us that our division can't expect any funds for employee training," he said. "I am so sorry." He was almost crying. I understood his problems and tried to stop him from being sorry.

I told him, "I understand the trouble you are facing very clearly. I am confident you can help your bank be back in business very soon. I want you to help the economies of both Japan and the world get back on track as quickly as possible." The man was still apologetic when he left my office.

The incident was a shock to me, even though I thought I was ready for things like this to happen. I knew companies were cutting back on expenditures for employee training. However, when the manager actually came to me to cancel the training, I felt shocked and anxious about the future of my new company. [18]

The incident made me appreciate further how important it is for me to help businesses develop great people and to help them solve difficult business issues.

---

[18] Cutback in training unfortunately also happened in the West. Actually, this is the best time to invest in people to help improve the company to grow for the future. Toyota is noted for not laying people off but to use the slow times to educate, train and build people's skills.

After all, people are the most important resource in any business.

I became even more aware of my societal responsibility to help develop employees, with not only strong business skills, but to also build their character.

I came to this conclusion by studying the mechanisms of the subprime loans and the demise of Lehman Brothers. These tragedies were caused by human and moral factors. If people who worked in the financial industry had the courage to reflect on the risky nature of the subprime products and speak up against putting them into the market, they would not have hurt their companies and the world economy. They should have said, "We can't sell the products because selling them would go against our ethics." No one was willing to take responsibility for selling the hazardous financial products.

The Harada Method Aims to Build Strong Character and Enhance Professional Skills at the Same Time.

I strongly believe that self-reliant people would have been able to make the right decisions on whether to sell subprime-related financial products or not, because they would have had a solid moral character. **When people pick strong goals, with purposes and values that serve not only themself but also serve others, their entire character changes.**

This does not mean that all successful people are entirely moral but we are saying that someone who is self-reliant is highly moral.

More specifically, a self-reliant person is an individual with great character. Self-reliant people care about the needs of society and willingly serve their community. They have the strong character necessary to balance societal and personal needs. They care about their personal needs and seek the best way to achieve their goals.

Excellent professional skills can harm society when not accompanied by a sense of morality. Someone who is not self-reliant might use their professional skills in a dangerous way because they lack morals. In the case of the financial industry, people without a strong character end up selling risky products they should not sell, like the subprime loans.

Enhance Your Spirit, Skills and Physical Condition

In Japan, there is an old saying: **"spirit, skills, and physical condition."** It highlights the three important factors needed for athletes to perform well. It also indicates the importance of harmonizing these factors to be a fully developed human being.

During the first four years of my career, I emphasized only one of the three factors, **skills**. I believed I could make my students strong by teaching them how—how to run fast, how to throw far and how to jump high. I was proud of my technical knowledge and wanted to show off what I knew to my students. When I look back now, I think that what I taught my students was too technical for them. Still, we achieved success, and despite not teaching all three factors.

In my fifth year, I was transferred to another junior high, where I would spend the next nine years. During this time, my focus changed from not only teaching skills but to also teach physical conditioning. I researched many athletes who were doing well at that time and realized that almost all of them were doing weight training.

This lesson was made clearer to me when I watched the 1988 Summer Olympic Games held in Seoul, South Korea. One of the worst events of the games was when a Canadian athlete failed a blood doping test and lost his gold medal. Why did he try doping even though he knew it was against the rules, unfair and bad for his health? The reason was simple: doping could enhance his physical strength so much that he could perform at his maximum effort, even during very demanding weightlifting sessions.

The lesson I took away from the doping incident was that weight training is a key to success, so I incorporated it (without the doping, of course) into exercise plans for my students. In those days, weight training was not popular in Japan, and many people had misconceptions about its effects. For example, many believed that too much weight training at a young age could stunt a child's growth. I closely examined the effects of weight training and created a new method to safely train younger people.

After weight training was brought into our exercise plan, my school became the champion out of 380 schools in the entire Osaka Prefecture. Still, I knew there was a long way to go before we would be the best in all of Japan.

Something Should be Added: a Daily Life

In my thirteenth year of teaching, I was transferred to Matsumushi Junior High School, located in the center of the city of Osaka. In those days, Matsumushi Junior High was in one of the toughest situations of all the schools in Osaka. This was reflected in the attitudes of its students. They lacked confidence, were lethargic and lived very difficult lives, so I decided to teach them how to improve their **spirits**.

Once again I looked for ideas from how Olympic gold medalists trained. I found that, especially in the United States, many athletes used psychological skills training (PST)[19] to improve their attitude, behavior and way of thinking.

Beginning in the 1980s, the United States' national teams hired professional coaches to teach PST. Japan fell behind, and even into the late 1990s, psychological skills training had still not been introduced.

I adapted PST to be easy and practical for junior high students, rearranging it to make it easier to teach. I

---

[19] Psychological Skills Training Program where imagery and goal setting are implemented.

named it the "mind-building system," or "PCDSS management cycle[20]."

I had finally found a way to improve the students' spirits. However, I soon realized that something was missing. I had reached my limit. The "spirit, skills and physical condition" point of view was very good, but it was not enough, especially for the students at Matsumushi, who lived in very harsh circumstances.

For example, there was one boy who had repeatedly been delinquent when he was in elementary school. After entering Matsumushi Junior High and becoming a member of my track and field team, he seemed to turn over a new leaf. As I got to know him, I realized he was honest, active, and full of drive. From Monday to Saturday, he practiced hard after school every day.

Every Monday morning, however, after a day without school or practice, he would come to school with many troubles. He came to school late because he could not get up on time after staying up late the night before. He was sometimes hurt because of fights he had with his friends on Sunday. Occasionally, the police took him into custody because he wandered around the city until midnight with some high school students.

Working with and observing the boy, I found the answer I was looking for. I realized what needed to be

---

[20] PCDSS is: Plan (think and write), Check (check yourself to see if you are ready), Do (work consistently), See (control yourself), and Share (help others)

added to "spirit, skills and physical condition." The key was to **control the quality of each day ("daily life")**.

Every student had 24 hours each day, and most of them spend eight hours a day at school. Some of them join school club activities and spend a couple more hours at school. What do they do with the other 14 hours? The 14 hours outside of school can deeply affect the 10 hours inside of school, and vice versa. Most teachers do not know what students are doing outside of school. My realization was that improving "spirit, skill and physical condition" should include all aspects of daily life—not only what students do when they are at school, but also what they do at home and in the neighborhoods too.

From years of trial and error, the truth finally came to me. By harmonizing "spirit, skill, physical condition and daily life (the four aspects)," you are enabled to manage your life by yourself. This is what being self-reliant is all about.

Improving the four aspects - spirit, skill, physical condition, and daily life - also applies to the adults who are working in society. **What you do when you leave the workplace greatly influences what you can achieve from nine to five at your workplace.** If you have troubles with your wife, it might disturb your concentration at your job. If you stay up late at night doing nothing but watching TV, it can harm your health, resulting in lower work performance. In order to do your best work, you have to be aware of how important all four aspects are.

The challenge, of course, is for managers to be able to motivate employees to improve their life outside of work without intruding on them. Mr. Harada's techniques will help employees make significant positive shifts in their non-work lives without the company overstepping its bounds.

As soon as the students in my Track and Field Club started to manage their life by themselves, their performances improved significantly. Even on Mondays, students would come to school on time. They paid more attention in class. Some students became leaders and played a major role in making the entire school better. They became more and more self-reliant.

Here is a short exercise to help you gauge how self-reliant you are. Each of the 33 words in the table is an aspect of self-reliance. For each word, give yourself a score of 1 to 10, with 10 being the highest.

#	Word	Score
1	Accountable	
2	Adaptable	
3	Authentic	
4	Brave	
5	Capable	
6	Caring	
7	Confident	
8	Creative	
9	Determined	
10	Ethical	
11	Empowered	
12	Flexible	
13	Highly skilled	
14	Honest	
15	Imaginative	
16	Independent	

#	Word	Score
17	Innovative	
18	Inspired	
19	Inquisitive	
20	Knowledgeable	
21	Motivated	
22	Organized	
23	Personable	
24	Prepared	
25	Proactive	
26	Realistic	
27	Responsible	
28	Self-managed	
29	Strategic	
30	Strong willed	
31	Supportive	
32	Trustworthy	
33	Visionary	

How Can You Become More Self-Reliant?

When you finish the above exercise, go back and take the lowest ten scores and think of ways to move your score up to a 10. For example, if I scored myself a 7 for "Realistic," my comment for how to improve might be "Stop day dreaming." If I rated myself a 5 for "Prepared," I might right, "Adhere exactly to the Harada Method then I will always be better prepared."

	Word	How to Improve
1		
2		
3		
4		
5		
6		
7		
8		
9		
10		

Hold onto your answers because you will use this list later when you are determining your tasks and daily routines.

A few years ago, I had a gardener named Savand who was born in Cambodia. I think of him as an example who was very self-reliant in his life. Savand would occasionally work around my house during the spring, summer and fall. To survive in the winter, he would go into the forest just outside of Portland and look for mushrooms to sell to local chefs.

Savand would gather the almond-scented matsutake mushrooms, for which Japanese gourmets will pay almost any price. He knew where to find the mushrooms among the pine trees and how to pick them. From his knowledge and skill, Savand was able to support himself and his family during the winter months. I think Savand is a good example of someone who is self-reliant — able to switch jobs and skills to support his family.

Why is Serving Others Important?

"The purpose in life is to serve others and do something of value."
- Temple Grandin, Ph.D.

A very important key to being successful with the method is to learn the importance of serving others. Serving others gives you a balance to achieve your goal and helps develop your character. Harada's idea that service to others is an important part of attaining success took me some time to understand. In America, we come from a culture that fosters the individual to succeed on his or her own. We are "rugged individualists," a legacy of the Wild West mentality. Sure, we give to charity and are good to our families and friends, but we are taught to be fiercely competitive in the world of business. It is fine to be fiercely competitive to motivate you to succeed and grow, but you should include others in your ambition. I like the idea of "win-win."

You do not need to serve others so that you can get something back. When you serve others, the quality of that act does something very beneficial to you. In fact, the more you focus on serving others, the greater your life experiences will be.

A mother does not serve her child with the thought of getting anything back. A mother just loves the child, serves the child well and is grateful when the child grows up to be an outstanding person.

When You Serve Others Well, You Break Own Your Own Limitations

After I started to publish the Productivity newsletter in 1980, I received a telephone call from Joe Snyder, an independent consultant, who congratulated me for publishing the newsletter. He felt it was very important for American industry to understand the meaning of productivity and to become more productive. He said, "Norman, I like what you do and I want to help you. What do you need?" I don't know about you, but I rarely ever heard this from another person - especially someone I had never met.

At the time, I was planning my first Productivity conference to be run in New York City. I said, "Joe, I need keynote speakers. I need great people to attract attendees. I would love to get a CEO of a major corporation, a labor leader and a politician." Joe said, "Let me work on it." Within days, he called back and said "Norman, I got Michael Rose, the CEO of Holiday Inns, and Don Ephlin, second in command in the United Automobile Worker's union (UAW) in charge of the Ford Motor Company account. My editor's brother worked for Stanley Lundine, congressman in upstate New York, who also keynoted the conference. Having these keynote speakers helped me attract leaders and practitioners from industry and our first conference was a great success.

Amazingly, Joe never asked anything from me. He just liked what we did and wanted to help. Joe later invited me to meet with him at the corporate office of the Chase Manhattan Bank in New York City to meet some of the senior managers. Joe was a consultant to the President of the Bank. It was a miracle, for I had high aspirations but knew really no one at the top of industry.

I do believe in the adage, "As ye sow, so shall ye reap." It is also called Karma. But the real challenge is to do things for the betterment of others without thinking of receiving anything back. Giving makes you stronger. Giving brings you pleasure - real happiness.[21]

---

[21] I am reading The How of Happiness: A New Approach to Getting the Life You Want by Sonja Lyubomirsky. In

My eldest daughter, Phillis, donates her time and once a week teaching aerobics to a group of senior citizens in Naples, Florida. They love her and she loves to do it. I have to figure out how to do something similar, to be like her and Joe Synder, to just serve.

Ritsuo Shingo, Dr. Shigeo Shingo's son, was President of Toyota Motors, China and President of Hino Motors, China. I have known Ritsuo for many years and recently asked him to share with me what serving others and being self-reliant meant to him.

"As their leader, I always tried to be honest and fair in all my relationships with my staff. From the bottom of my heart I wanted to make sure that people were taken care of in the best possible way. It was through a "heart to heart" relationship not a "brain to brain" relationship.

Whenever I did something for another person I never expected to get anything in return. I never thought about what I would get out of it. I also tried to treat people as if we were all on the same level. I did not want to look at people as if I was on a higher level than they were. I did not look down on people. Whenever I told people what to do I also told them why they should do it.

The above was my basic attitude in relating with people. It was not easy but I continued to try to do it."

Mr. Harada wants us to learn how to be successful, and he knows that we must break down our

---

this wonderful book you will see how setting goals and serving others are the prime ways to become and stay happy.

old perceptions about how things should be done in order to do the right things that will help you succeed. Now, we also know how hard it is to break habits, but we must do that. We break old habits by establishing new positive ones, and one way to do this is to serve others meaningfully.

Mr. Harada is now the president of a very successful consulting company in Japan and yet every day when he goes home he cleans the toilet and at work he cleans his associates' desks and arranges their shoes. He does this to help others but also because he knows that by doing humbling things for others it will build his character. It will help him to sustain his efforts to attain his goals, no matter how difficult those goals might be.

When Mr. Harada teaches, he wants everyone to pick things they can do to serve others at work and at home. He wants them to look for things that others are doing that they might not like to do or tend to avoid doing.

Mr. Harada calls the acts of service "indirect-efforts." On the other hand, actions like calling 15 clients a day or delivering 300 fliers a day are called "direct efforts." In the Harada Method, indirect efforts can improve your character, and it is your strong character that will drive you forward to achieve your goals and maximize your skills and potentials. The indirect efforts will lead to better results from the direct efforts.

Service to others can strengthen your mind. In other words, it will train you to be more patient. You may think that cleaning or washing dishes are nothing but an easy job to do, but how about if you continue cleaning for

30 days, a year, or a life? In fact, Mr. Harada wants you to establish a new pattern of service and then do it for 1000 days to make sure that it is ingrained deeply inside you. Often, we do things for a short while and then go back to our "old way of doing things." We want you to be successful and know that it will only come from making your new habits lasting.

One of Harada's students who was number one in her sport among all Japanese shared the key to her success. A reporter from a track magazine asked her, "Why do you think you won the tournament?" She proudly said, "I won because I washed the dishes every day for a year. I did not skip once. No exceptions."

How can washing dishes for a year be the most important thing she did to win the tournament? Washing dishes helped to develop her character. It helped her focus on serving others. It helped her to be consistent every day in her practice. Athletes know that if they miss even one day of practice it could be detrimental to honing their skills.

The following case study is an example of how service benefits others as well as the person doing the serving.

Case Study - Improving Sales at an Insurance Company

A woman who worked at an insurance company as a salesperson was having a very difficult time attracting customers. She was very shy when she came to work and did not have the confidence required to make sales.

One day, the woman attended a Harada Method workshop put on by the company called "The Humanity Improvement Workshop." At the workshop, the woman learned how to set goals in the Harada way. She was intrigued by the teachings and wanted to learn more. After the workshop, she went to watch the track and field practices at Matsumushi Junior High School, where Mr. Harada once coached.

By then, Harada had left the school to become a business consultant, but his teachings and methodology were still being used at the school. The Harada Method was ingrained into the school culture and the Matsumushi students worked very hard. They trained by their own initiative, without receiving any orders from the teachers.

Inspired by the intensity of the students desire to succeed, the woman decided that she wanted to become the No. 1 salesperson in her company, even though she did not have a successful track record.

One of the lessons the woman learned from taking Harada's seminar and visiting Matsumushi was the importance of serving others. As one of her routines, she elected to clean up the street near her office every morning.

The act of cleaning every morning made a big change in the woman's attitude as well as her success as a salesperson. In one month, she achieved her new sales goal and eventually became the third best salesperson out of 400 in the company.

Why was the woman so successful? This is how she explained her success: "At first I felt a little embarrassed and shy when I cleaned up the street wearing the company's uniform. However, soon thereafter, I started to exchange greetings with the neighbors and the people walking by to work. I became less embarrassed and got used to cleaning up the area. Over time, the people passing by started to thank me for the cleaning activities. 'You've worked hard since early in the morning,' they would say."

"My confidence improved and then a feeling of gratitude came to my mind. I realized now I could do much better when I talked with customers on the phone. In the past, I would simply read parts of our manual, but now I can talk with them directly from my heart."

The woman's branch manager was impressed. "It seems to me that cleaning up for the neighbors has enhanced the spirit of teamwork and given a fresh new attitude to everyone around," he said. "Our company's connection with the people living in the community has strengthened and I believe that the number of people who come to our branch has increased three times as much as before."

By studying the Harada Method, the woman learned how to develop her character through serving others. She did not begin cleaning the neighborhood just to obtain new sales. Before she could be a successful salesperson, she needed to change her attitude. Once she did that, the new sales came.

Chapter 4 – Select Your Main Goal – The Long-Term Goal Setting Form

"It's supposed to be hard. If it wasn't hard, everyone would do it. The hard is what makes it great."
-Tom Hanks in A League of Their Own

We will now take you through the steps to complete the Harada Long-Term Goal Setting Form. Although it is called the long-term form, it can also be an excellent tool for setting and achieving short-term goals as well. You could use it for an important goal you want to attain in the next two weeks or the next month.

Below is illustrated the top portion of the form. As you see, this is an example from one person Mr. Harada taught in Japan, named Takumi Tahara:

	Harada Method Long-Term Goal Form				
Name	Takumi Tahara	Start Date	4/1/2011	Best goal target date	4/30/2011
Everyday service to family	I clean the bathroom at home before leaving for work	Everyday service to workplace	I clean the company entrance before starting work		

Section: Top Line

On the top line write your name and the date that you plan to get started workings towards your goal. Next, indicate the date when you hope to attain your goal.

Section: Service to Others

As we talked about in the proceeding chapter, service is an important component of the Harada Method. Serving others at work and at home teaches you humility, and builds stronger relationships. Harada wants you to understand that self-reliance and personal success come when you gain full support from your family, friends and business associates. To gain other's support, you must first show your ability to serve others.

Mr. Harada could work with his students to improve at school, but he knew that their home life had a great affect on the overall performance of the students. Mr. Harada didn't ask his students' parents to change, he asked his students to start to make changes to their home environments by doing something positive every day at home. As the students did things differently at home, serving others, miraculously the home environment changed for the better.

Write in the section "Everyday service to family" what you will do to serve your family differently to have a positive effect on their lives. Mr. Harada, for example, cleans the bathroom at his house. In the box on the right of the form, write what you will do every day as a service at your workplace. This can be something simple, just try to make it something that will make things easier or better for others. The whole idea of everyday service is to help you change some of your patterns. You are not asking others to change; by doing different things to serve others you will change.

Name	Mr. Hideki Morikawa	Decision date (today) 6/5/11	Best goal target date 7/1/11
Service to others What will you do	(Family) & everyday I wash dishes after dinner everyday.	(Workplace) & everyday I clean the company restroom	

Goal Setting

The major step for filling out your long-term form is to pick your goal – this should be something you want to work for and will make a major difference in your life. It can be a big goal for your current job or a big change you want to make that might lead to a new job or career, but it should lead to you achieving a more successful life. It is not easy to pick a goal, but you can do it. Sometimes this is what people struggle the most, but it is important. So spend some time really thinking about your life plans and goals.

Know Clearly Why You Want to Achieve Your Goal

Begin the process by dreaming what you want to do in life to have the best possible life. Think of a strong purpose for your goal, something that you can really get excited and passionate about. Understand why you want to reach this goal. When people understand why they want to achieve their goal, they become more motivated. Look at the determination of an Olympic athlete. They know the value of winning a gold medal, and they are willing to put in the extreme effort to attain it.

Goal Setting	By the 1st of July, I will receive an award from the headquarters for being an excellent store manager who accomplished sales of $160,000 in June and I will travel abroad with my family	By the 1st of July the surrounding community will love my store for providing high-quality customer services

When I was a lot younger, I had no idea what I wanted to do in life. I went to school like everyone else but had no ambition. I had nothing to motivate me to succeed - nothing to motivate me to do my homework, nothing for me to focus on. I hated school because I didn't see any reason for what I was being taught. I was not good a student. I never received an "A," not one outstanding mark in any subject until the 10th grade. I had no vision for my life. Luckily, I did go off to college but still didn't know what I wanted to do. I studied to be an accountant because my father and brother were accountants. I did not like being an accountant, and, fortunately, I left accounting just three years after graduating from college and eventually became a publisher, writer, teacher and lecturer – a career I am very passionate and excited about.

In contrast, Jonathan Puzzo, son of Carmen Puzzo a business associate of mine, is 11 years old and has decided to be an orthopedic doctor when he grows up. Knowing what he wants to be gives Jonathan a powerful focus on what to study. I believe it is central to your success in life to know exactly what you want to do in the future.

In one of my classes at Portland State University, I asked around 40 graduate students if they had a goal – something to strive for to be successful in life. Not one hand went up. Not one student was willing to admit that they had a goal. They wanted to get their degree. They then were all hopeful that a company would give them a job after graduating. I am sure they wanted a good job, an interesting position, but they were going to leave that up to their future company. With the Harada Method, you can be the "master of your own fate." You pick a strong goal and then go after it. You will be amazed how this works when you take an interview for a job and you can tell the interviewer of your long-term desire and how it will benefit the company.

Adam, a young man who recently interned with me, graduated in June 2012. He wants to be involved in international management. He is hopeful that a company will hire him and give him something interesting to do. I hope he will get what he wants, but to me it is much better if Adam can be much more specific on what he wants to do in international management, that he can tell a company, He can say something like, "I would like to use my Chinese language ability to help you communicate with your suppliers in China, and in the future be able to help you carefully build up a great network of suppliers in the world."

Without a clear goal, you will be unable to focus your full attention on being successful. As you try to figure out what goal to pick, look for opportunities that exist in your company. You want your goal to advance your career and to also be aligned with the success of your company.

Take Advantage of Your Education and Prepare Yourself to Succeed in a Tough Job Market

Years past, almost every college graduate was able to obtain a job upon graduation, but no longer. A recent article in a newspaper described the difficulties college graduates are having as they try to find work.

> **"The college class of 2012 is in for a rude welcome to the world of work. A weak labor market already has left half of young college graduates either jobless or underemployed in positions that don't fully use their skills and knowledge."**
> **- From "One in Two New Graduates Are Jobless or Underemployed" - By Hope Yen, Associated Press, April 22, 2012**

Many of my students at Portland State University are only focused on graduating with a degree, thinking that the degree will get them a good job. Very few people realize that the world of employment opportunities has changed. Many, do not, in my opinion, put in the necessary effort to fully take advantage of what college has to offer. They are spending tens of thousands of dollars for an education, but not fully understanding the very simple formula, "input equals output."

Once you have your "goal" you can really put in the effort to learn and gain the skills needed to be successful. When you pick a goal that will develop you to your fullest capability and give you a skill that is needed in society, you are virtually guaranteed to be successful in life.

The Harada Method uses a sports analogy to help you pick your goal. As an example, visualize yourself as an athlete wanting to be the best javelin thrower in the world. Your goal might be to break the past world record of 98.48M, set by Jan Telezny in 1996.[22] You now know

---

[22] At the 2012 London Olympics Keshorn, Walcott from Trinidad and Tobago won the men's gold medal by

what your target is to succeed and from here you can begin to take the necessary steps. At work, you need the same kind of target as an athlete. Just like the javelin thrower, you need to pick your goal and decide what you have to do to reach it.

Right now, your work might be boring and repetitive. You might come to work every day dying for Friday to arrive, but it doesn't have to be that way. Work can be interesting -really exciting - once you pick a goal and begin to work towards achieving that goal.

In fact, the work you are doing right now, even if boring, can be a stepping-stone for a great future. Say you are doing a very simple repetitive task such as turning ten bolts on every car. It is boring work, but you can transform your attitude. Just look around your job and find small things to improve that will make your work easier and more interesting. Once you can perfect the work you are doing, no matter how boring, you will then be able to move on to the next step possibly learning how to build an engine. With a goal, you can begin to do what you need to do to reach that goal. You might go to night school. You might ask someone at work to be your mentor. There are so many variables to lead you to achieving your goal.

At UniQlo, the clothing store in Japan, I once watched a clerk quickly fold shirts, sweaters and other clothing handled by customers. She was taught and practiced to fold the clothing very, very quickly and to put them back very neatly on the shelves. UniQlo is noted for

---

throwing the javelin 84.58m while Barbora Spotakova from the Czech Republic threw 69.55m.

the outstanding appearance of their merchandise in the store. The clerk was an expert in folding. It was an important part of her job to fold clothing quickly, but it also became a competitive game between clerks. I just felt that folding shirts with her competitive attitude, wanting the product to look perfectly for the customer, took away the boredom from the job.

It's important to remember that all work, if necessary, is good work. That doesn't mean you have to do the same thing for the rest of your life. You might be washing dishes now, but you should have the opportunity to do something else in the future and the sooner the better.

Don't Wait for Your Manager to Give You the Opportunity to Grow

The problem for most people is that they are waiting for their boss to give them the opportunity to grow and try new things. It might not happen. Many managers are continually pressured to get the work out and find very little time to help their employees advance.

The Harada Method is unique because the catalyst for your growth is you, not your manager or anyone else. Managers should be there to facilitate and help their employees improve. If you don't have a manager to challenge you, then I advise you to find a coach or a good friend who can help you stay on the path you selected for yourself. To me, one of the prime roles of a manager is to help people develop themselves to their fullest capability. The manager should act like a coach, helping every employee build new skills.

You need to see yourself becoming an artisan, highly skilled at something you would like to do, in a discipline that serves both you and others. It might be a lathe operator or a supply-chain manager looking after overseas operations or an automobile mechanic able to repair Ferrari automobiles or whatever you can envision that will excite you. Pick something you want to be the best at in the world.

Try to visualize, dreaming, that you already achieved your goal, and then work backward from the future to the present reviewing the steps you took to get there. Once you have the vision of your future self, you just have to reconstruct what you already did to attain your success. Try it. It works!

Harada tells us that we can all be successful if we are willing to pick a meaningful goal and put in the effort to attain it.

Here's a quick exercise that can help you start to define your goal. Take a sheet of paper and write down 50 positive things about yourself. Write down those things that you were successful doing in the past. Now look at the list and select 10 possible future goals, based on your past successes, that you think you would give you an interesting and exciting life. Then show the list to your family and friends to get their feedback. Review your list until you can pick one thing to become your goal.

Harada Value Management: Plan, Think, Write

Every Successful Person Has a Script for Their Own Success

Success is no accident. We analyzed many important historical figures, successful people and Olympic gold medalists and their coaches, to find out what made them great. We found that most of them achieved their success by the power of will. They made a conscious decision to become successful from the very beginning. They created a script to guide their actions. The Harada Long-Term Goal Form can be your script for reaching your goal.

Add Meaning to Your Job

The Harada Long-Term Goal Form is used to both enhance your character and to improve your job performance. This sheet of paper also states the techniques necessary to achieve your goals. The form is also used to help you to improve your way of thinking and to develop your attitude of self-reliance.

In an ordinary goal management system, you are normally given a goal by your boss along with ways to measures your performance in attaining those goals. **This puts a lot of pressure on you to meet someone else's perception of what you should achieve. You have a quota, - the goal that you must achieve no matter what.** You might not feel the need for any creativity, autonomy, or independence as long as you see the goal as a number or quota forced upon you by someone else. Reaching your quota is just a numerical achievement. It does not develop you as a self-reliant person.

The Harada Method teaches you that "success" means to achieve a goal that is valuable and worthwhile to you. Your attitude is important. As you complete the Harada Long-Term Goal Form, you will realize that the work you are doing is something that is practical and can lead to future benefits.

Think of this as an exciting opportunity to carefully examine yourself as you complete the form. Please be honest and write what you think. In each section on the form, write as many ideas as possible. The more seriously you take developing your goal, the more attainable your life's script will become.

Two Keys to Setting Your Goal:

First Key: Is the Goal Valuable and Worthwhile for You?

If the goal is valuable for you, it will excite and motivate you. It will also bring you a sense of purpose and mission. This will help you overcome the difficulties that you may face in the process of reaching your goal.

Second Key: Is the Goal Measurable and Quantifiable Enough that You Will Be Able to Use the Measures to Guide Your Successful Efforts?

You want to know that you are on track, that you are staying on your schedule to attain your target. How do you know that you are getting close to achieving your goal? You need some kinds of measurement. If you want to be a teacher, you would explore the courses necessary to take at college to get your teaching degree. If you want to be the best salesman in your company, you can set very specific sales goals.

Many people will be tempted to write a goal like this: "I will do my best in sales in June." "Do my best" is a very subjective description, and this kind of effort cannot be easily measured or quantified. It's much better to say, "I will accomplish $200,000 in sales in June."

By setting a goal that is measurable and quantifiable, you and others can judge whether you achieve your goal. When other people can easily understand your measurable and quantifiable goal, they can help you in concrete ways.

Sometimes it is hard to set a goal that is measurable and quantifiable. We come up with goals like, "We will be the best baseball team." or "I will be a good father to my kids." Instead, you should choose something like "We will finish in first place in the league" or "I will not work Saturdays so I can spend the children." Then you have something specific to judge your progress.

Why do most people not set goals to drive them forward? Maybe it is the fear of failure that has been drummed into so many. We think if we don't set any goals then we can't fail. But that is foolish, for everyone wants to succeed in life.

We have just started to fill out the long-term goal setting form and will continue in the next upcoming

SELECT YOUR MAIN GOAL

chapters. The following is an example of the top part of the form.

Harada's Goal Setting form

Name	Mr. Takumi Tahara		Decision date April 1, 2012	Best goal target date April 30, 2012
Service to others What will you do	(Family) & everyday.) I clean restroom before leaving to work.		(Workplace) & everyday) I clean the company entrance before starting to work.	
Goal Setting	By the 30ᵗʰ of April Heisei 22, I will achieve $250,000 in April sales and receive an incentive for that achievement.		By the 30ᵗʰ of April Heisei 22, I will achieve $250,000 in April sales and be able to provide even better quality of customer service.	
Goals	Highest goal:	I will accomplish $300,000 in sales in April!		
	Intermediate	I will accomplish $200,000 in sales in April!		
	Confident or easiest goal	I will accomplish $150,000 in sales in April!		
	Current capability	I will accomplish $250,000 in sales in April!		
Milestone goal	Confident → Date April 23, 2012		Intermediate date → Date April 27, 2012	
Value and purpose of your goals: four perspectives on the goals List as many as you can.	Tangible: My company's sale increases My salary gets raised. Customer satisfaction increases I receive some incentives My customers receive higher quality service My management skill will be developed My employees receive some incentives I will be able to save to start my own business Society · Others ·················· For yourself ·················· My family members become vivid and happy. Attain a sense of confidence My customers have a quality time in peace. Being fulfilled as an individual My employees are motivated for work. I'm more motivated to work My employees become more confident Be positive toward myself The shopping street thrives. The food industry as a whole thrives. Intangible: I will be more confident in my work			
Goals in process	April 10ᵗʰ $80,000 in store sales > April 18ᵗʰ $160,000 in store sales > April 25ᵗʰ $200,000 in store sales			

Chapter 5 - Select Your Goals to Monitor Your Performance

"You don't always get what you wish for, you get what you work for " - Unknown

We must be firm with ourselves if we want to set goals and to achieve them, so it is vital that we set a completion or target date. In 1961, President Kennedy said the U.S. would send a man to the moon by the end of the decade, and Neil Armstrong's[23] boot clomped down onto the lunar dirt on July 20, 1969. Setting a completion date gives you powerful motivation to force you to focus on attaining your goal.

Your attitude should be that you will set a realistic completion date and you "must" attain the goal on or before that date. There is no excuse and no exception. There is no point in setting goals without a completion date. Goals without dates are just dreams. An athlete knows when the game will be played and must be prepared to be at top form on that exact date. When you pick a goal, you should also pick an exact date when you want to attain it.

The Harada Method completely separates dreams and goals. Dreams are just dreams. You hope they will come true, but instead of pursuing them you just feel sorry for yourself when they do not materialize. Goals are more serious and practical than dreams. You have to

---

[23] Neil Armstrong died August 25, 2012 at the age of 82.

prepare yourself for achieving them. It is great to have a vision of what is possible for you, but when you decide what you really want, you convert those dreams into attainable goals.

Thus, once you set the completion date for your goal, it gives you real motivation to attain them. The completion date motivates you to put into action what you have planned.

Setting Different Goal Levels - The Milestone Goals

In the Harada Method we set four kinds of goals: highest goal, intermediate or moderate goal, confident or easiest goal and what you think you can do with your current capability. When you have a series of goals, you are preparing to stretch yourself.

Goals			
	Highest goal	I will accomplish $300,000 sales in April!	Date
	Intermediate goal	I will accomplish $200,000 sales in April	Date
	Confident goal	I will accomplish $150,000 sales in April.	Date
	Current capability	I can make $250,000 sales in April	Date

Highest Goal

Your highest goal should stretch your capabilities a lot. It should be very difficult for you to achieve but also reachable if you dedicate all of your strength to it and someone helps you.

Example 1: If I were an athlete throwing the shot put, I would know that the world record is 23.12 meters

(75 feet 10.2 inches) set in 1990 by Randy Barnes.[24] Therefore, I would set my sights on coming close to or exceeding 23.12 meters. That would be my highest goal.

Example 2: If I were a salesman and I sold $100,000 in products last month, and I knew that the best salesman in the company sold $160,000, I might set my best goal for the coming month to be $160,000 or more.

Example 3: I want to be "The best teacher in the West teaching managers and teachers how to teach employees and students how to be successful in life." I want to teach managers how to be great managers and I want to teach teachers how to be great teachers. I think I can accomplish this by teaching them the Harada Method. Now, my challenge is to quantify this goal so that I can measure my rate of success. "I will teach 1000 managers and teachers in the next 12 months how to teach the Harada Method."

Confident or Easiest Goal

Look back at your past experiences and successes. Drawing on that experience, think of a goal that seems easy for you to achieve. This is called the confident (easiest) goal. It is a minimal goal that you can achieve.

---

[24] Natalya Lisovskaya, Soviet Union, in June 7, 1987 threw the shot put 22.63 meters, 74 feet 2.9 inches. In open competitions the men's shot weighs 7.260 kilograms (16.01 lbs), and the women's shot weighs 4 kilograms (8.8 lbs)

Example 1: Since I can throw the shot put 15.4 meters in practice, I feel that I can easily repeat this in competition.

Example 2: Last month I sold $100,000 in sales and I feel confident that I can easily repeat that amount this month.

Example 3: I plan to run a one-week workshop in September and I am confident that I will attract 5 managers to attend. I had five attend my last workshop.

Intermediate Goal or Moderate Goal

The intermediate (moderate) goal is something that seems challenging to achieve but not too difficult. This could be half-way between what you feel is easy and what you call your highest goal.

Example 1: With hard practice, I feel that I will be able to throw the shot put 19.2 meters at the end of the month.

Example 2: I have a strategic plan to attract new customers and I feel that I will be able to sell $130,000 this month.

Example 3. With a new marketing plan, I will be able to attract 7 attendees to my workshop.

Current Capability

After you have set the highest goal, the easiest goal and the intermediate goal, set the goal for the current capability in that range. The current capability is a goal that, if you put in the extra effort and follow your growth plan, you are most likely to achieve this coming month.

Example 1: I am hopeful that I can develop an excellent training process that will build up my muscles and allow me to throw the shot put at 21.5 meters this month.

Example 2: With really hard work, my goal is to sell at least $120,000 this month.

Example 3: I will think of new ways of marketing and plan to attract 10 attendees this month.

Use the Goal Types to Understand Your Capabilities

Experienced goal achievers can set goals and give in-depth reasons why their goals are important and attainable. They use past data, or analyze external environment before setting goals. They give their full attention to the goals. For me to be the best teacher of the Harada Method, I have to be totally committed to learning, writing about and teaching the process. People who are chronic underachievers unfortunately do not make real commitments. They set goals that are nothing but a blind guesses. By setting goals within an achievable range or steps, you will come to realize what your maximum capability is and what you can easily attain with only a minimum effort on your part.

The four types of goals help you determine what

you are capable of accomplishing. By writing down the four goal levels, you now can see what you have to do to attain each one. You can then work out your detailed plans and predict what kind of effort is required to achieve these goals. These are the steps for setting the levels:

1. Pick your highest possible goal

2. State what you are absolutely confident you can attain.

3. The intermediate goal is normally not that far from the highest goal.

4. This time - you feel very good that with a little bit more effort you can attain this goal. You know that this goal is within your capability and you feel very confident that you can achieve it.

5. The confident goal is based on what you achieved in the past that you can do again. It is your baseline.

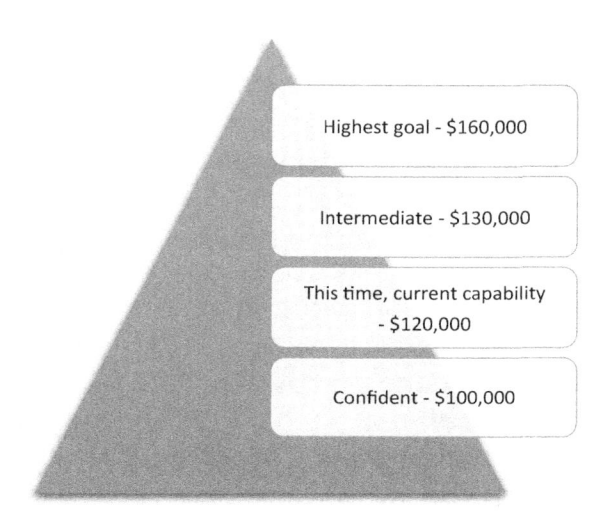

- Highest goal - $160,000
- Intermediate - $130,000
- This time, current capability - $120,000
- Confident - $100,000

In this example, you decide you can achieve at least $100,000 and at most $160,000. When you set the goal within your possibility of achieving it, your image of success will become clearer, and the possibility of achieving it becomes higher.

Another Example of Goal Levels

When one of Harada's student athletes set the goal for All-Japan Championships, she set her goals like this:

Highest Goal: No.1 in Japan
Intermediate Goal: No. 3 in Japan
This time: No. 8 in Japan
Confident Goal: No. 30 in Japan

At that time, 50 junior high shot-putters attended the championship, so if the student were to pick a goal from the "top of her head," she might have set her goal to finish No. 15 in Japan. But Harada taught her to set each goal from the difficulty level point of view, so she set her intermediate goal to be "No. 3 in Japan."

In summary, the **highest goal** means the most difficult but you want to challenge yourself. The **confident goal** means the least difficult to achieve. The **intermediate goal** means hard to reach, but not as difficult as the highest goal. **This time** means the goal that you believe you can achieve right now.

Note that the completion date is the same for each of the four goals. You start out by setting the completion date and then set the four levels of goals within that time frame. People sometimes misunderstand and think that the highest goal is the long-term goal, and the confident or the goal for this time is like a short-term goal.

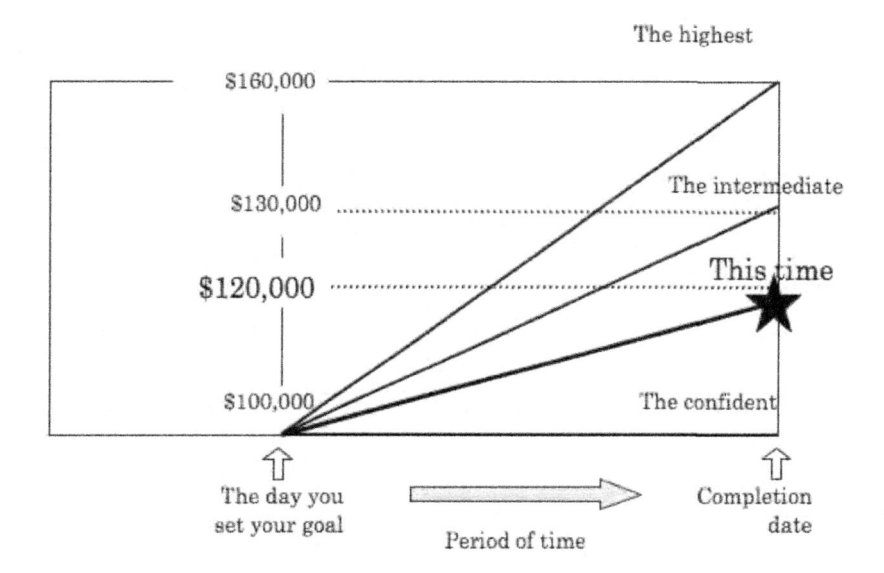

```
$160,000 ─── The highest
$130,000 ····· The intermediate
$120,000 ····· This time ★
$100,000 ───── The confident
↑ The day you set your goal      Period of time →      ↑ Completion date
```

Determination Plus Character Make You Successful

To become a sports champion you must have a deep conviction to win, a strong belief and determination in your ability to learn how to do it. You must build your physical skills, develop a strong mind and sustain your efforts until your goal is achieved.

Malcolm Gladwell, the author of Outliers, said that virtually every great master spent at least 10,000 hours developing themselves and their skill. We are born with a certain talent level, and if we don't develop it, it will go to waste. If you are going to put 10,000 hours into something, why not put it into building some skill that you can use to serve others and have a great life? Nothing of value comes without effort. Sure, you could win the lottery but your odds of doing that is one out of a million or something like that. If you pick a goal and work at it, you have a much better chance to be successful and you can have a lot of fun in the process.

    When people come to work they cannot isolate themselves from their troubles at home, even though we would like them to. We want them to concentrate, but in their minds they are worried about their children or spouse, etc. Managers rarely get involved with someone's home life but there are things that you can teach and encourage people to do to improve their home environment. The simple act of washing dishes at home every night and cleaning daily the practice field after school helps build the very strong character needed to sustain your efforts.

Chapter 6 - Set Milestone Goals

"Ability may get you to the top, but it takes character to keep you there."
- John Wooden, Basketball Coach

Milestone goals along path to goal	$48,000 in store sales by June 12th	$120,000 store sales by June 22nd
	$160,000 store sales by July 1st	

Set Your Goals in Process

It would be nice if you could reach all your goals at once, without getting lost in the process of pursuing them. However, you might get frustrated in the middle of pursuing a goal because you cannot see your progress. You may not always know what is right or wrong when you are in the middle of doing something. To overcome this, write down some measurable milestone goals between the time you start working towards your goal and your goal due date to help motivate you to stay on track.

Examples of milestone goals for a salesperson who wants to sell $160,000 worth of products in June:

Milestone 1: I will accomplish $48,000 in sales by June 12th.

Milestone 2: I will accomplish $120,000 in sales by June 22nd.

Milestone 3: I will accomplish $160,000 in sales by July 1st.

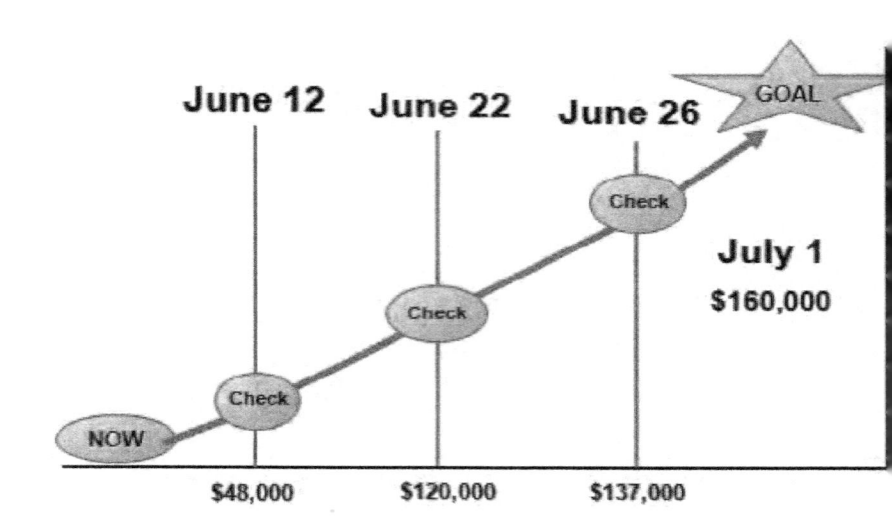

```
June 12    June 22    June 26    GOAL
                                 
                          Check
                                  July 1
                   Check          $160,000
         Check
  NOW
  $48,000    $120,000   $137,000
```

Steps to Set Your Milestone Goals

1. Divide your goal into measurable sections. Think of milestone goals as steps between now and the future.

2. Set at least three milestone goals. You can set more than three if you choose.

3. Give each milestone goal a date when you want to check your progress and action plans.

4. If you are behind your schedule, modify your actions and plans to get back on track. DO NOT reset your goals downward.

Case Study - Cosmo[25] Securities Co., Ltd.

In 2004, Cosmo Securities had a hard time with aftereffects of the burst economic bubble. To survive, the company had to downsize, which created a harsh atmosphere in the company. Most of the employees felt tired and restless, fearing further layoffs and even a possible shutdown.

Mr. Moriyama, the president of Cosmo, decided to rebuild the company by training employees using the Harada Method. Takashi Harada was already famous for training employees of UniQlo, a casual wear manufacturer and retailer with 859 stores worldwide.

The Harada Method employee-training program started in 2004. Harada trained all of the employees of Cosmo, a total of 1200 people The program led to some outstanding results for Cosmo and the amount of assets deposited increased at many branches.

Mr. Moriyama wanted further improvement, so the company launched a study group called "Cosmo Juku" or "Cosmo study group." All of the top executives, branch managers (including Mr. Moriyama himself) joined the study group. They met one evening a month to study leadership and the Harada Method. The group members

---

[25] Cosmo Securities merged with and is 100% owned by Iwai Securities.

practiced completing their individual Long-Term Goal Forms, the Routine Check Sheet, and their Harada Diaries in order to be able to train all of their employees.

Three years later, Mr. Moriyama saw that Cosmo's business performances and productivity had improved, and also the culture of the company was much better.

Using the Harada Method, Cosmo created a powerful management system of its own. With the system Cosmo was able to enhance both business performance and their employees self-reliant attitude at the same time.

Cosmo's executive secretary, Mr. Okuda, trumpeted the results. "Before introducing the Harada Method," he said, "our motto was 'you are what your sales show.' We were a results-based company. However, many employees felt tired and were mentally worn out. I was one of them. I knew I was worn out and if I continued on that way I was going to destruct my family and myself. But Mr. Harada taught us the importance of respect for people and for being self-reliant. We realized we were able to improve relationships in the process on achieving our business goals. I am grateful to Mr. Harada for making us truly self-reliant."

Chapter 7- State Your Purposes and Values

"Love is the force that ignites spirit and binds teams together"
- Phil Jackson, former Bulls and Lakers Coach

The simplest principle of the Harada Method is:

Purposes Push You Toward Your Goals.

You place a great deal of importance on purposes when you set your goals. When you have a very strong purpose you will apply yourself more effectively to achieve your goals.

Principal Goals Come After Purposes

With the Harada Method, you must think of your purpose whenever you set a goal. You need to write down your underlying motivation for the things you want to do. For example, why do you want to earn $100,000 a year? Why do you want to sell 500 cars a month? Why do you want to get those tangible results? Why do you want to achieve your goals? Why do you want to be a better carpenter? Why do you want to be a corporate accountant? Why do you want to be a physician assistant?

The right reason will lead you to the right goal. Without understanding your purpose for wanting to

reach certain goals, you can tend to be preoccupied with tangible results and end up with a narrow-minded view that focuses only on you own benefits. Recognize that the deeper your purposes are that benefit both you and others; you will increase your motivation to succeed.

Setting and attaining new goals requires you to make changes in your life. It is not easy to change your habits or patterns unless you have a strong reason for doing so. Purposes act as a kind of energy that drives you right to your goals.

Knowing that your goal has value for others in addition to yourself should motivate you to pursue it with more determination. The deeper the purpose, the more meaningful it is and the easier it will be for you to attain. For example, when I was in the Army and my buddies were depending on me for their lives, I would never disappoint them - never. In the same way, when you have someone else depending on you, you are much more motivated. You think to yourself, "If I can attain my goal, I know my family will have a better life. My children can go to college and I will not let them down. They are depending on me to succeed, so I will be successful."

Intrinsic Goals

Anthony, my grandson, came to see me with a problem about his job. I wanted to help him so I gave him advice that I thought would be helpful. "Write down the things you learn during the day and I am sure you will be able to use those stories for a future book," I told him. I knew it was difficult to change the circumstances of his job so I wanted him to dig deeper and find things of value that would change his spirit. But, when he left, I knew he was not happy with the advice. What I didn't realize, until then, was that the advice was extrinsic, coming from me to him. Even though I thought it was good advice and should be helpful to him, it was not something that he came up with on his own and could internalize.

This is what happens often at work. The boss tells you what to do instead of presenting the problem to you and asking you to come up with a solution. When you can take ownership over the solution, and the boss agrees with you, you will be much more motivated at work. I hope I can do this with my future students and find ways of asking them instead of telling them how to solve problems.

Taiichi Ohno, the former Vice President of production at Toyota, would never tell people how to do things. He would only tell them what he wanted them to do. "You have six people in your department. See if you can do the work with only three." He would walk away and come back in three months to see what you did. He was a terror, but Toyota became one of the largest companies in the world as people were forced to continuously improve. They improved from their own creative ideas not being told how to do it by senior management.

The Harada Method helps you gain a deeper understanding of the values and purposes behind your goals. The Harada Method gives you a structure, but you decide what is important to you and the stronger your purpose the more motivated you will be to attain your goal. Write your purposes under four types - the more lines your write the more effective you will be:

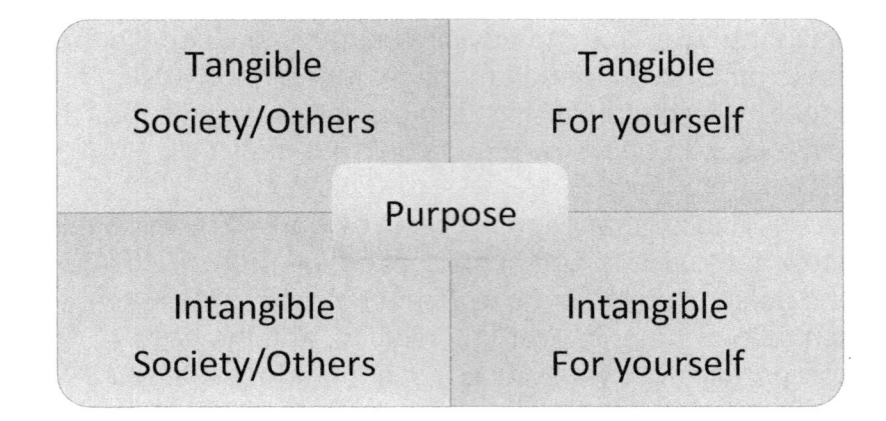

Tangible Society/Others	Tangible For yourself
Purpose	
Intangible Society/Others	Intangible For yourself

Tangible:

Society/Others: How attaining your goal will please others in a material or tangible way, e.g., "my wife will be able to buy a new couch," or "my division's profitability will improve."

For yourself: How attaining your goal will benefit you in a material or tangible way, e.g., "I will be able to take a vacation in the Caribbean." Other examples could include improving your skill development or getting a good annual evaluation.

Intangible:

Society/Others: These purposes improve the lives of those around you in a non-material way, e.g., "my boss will be very proud of my accomplishments and he will trust me more," or "I am helping my local community."

For yourself: These are purposes that make you feel better about yourself and develop your character as well, e.g., "I will be more confident," or "I will feel like I accomplished something."

In the "Values and Purposes" box on the Long-Term Goal Form, write as many tangible and intangible reasons why you want to achieve your goal as you can think of. Use the example below as a guide.

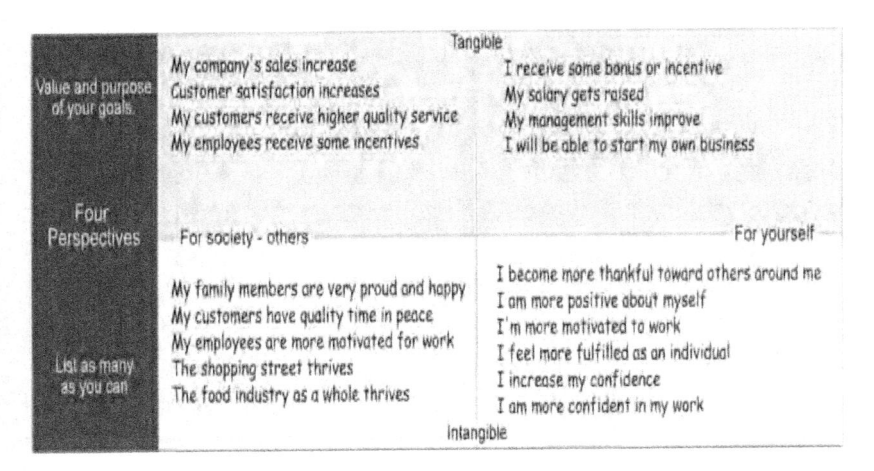

Value and purpose of your goals	Tangible	
	My company's sales increase	I receive some bonus or incentive
	Customer satisfaction increases	My salary gets raised
	My customers receive higher quality service	My management skills improve
	My employees receive some incentives	I will be able to start my own business
Four Perspectives	For society - others	For yourself
List as many as you can	My family members are very proud and happy	I become more thankful toward others around me
	My customers have quality time in peace	I am more positive about myself
	My employees are more motivated for work	I'm more motivated to work
	The shopping street thrives	I feel more fulfilled as an individual
	The food industry as a whole thrives	I increase my confidence
		I am more confident in my work
	Intangible	

Once again, the clearer your goal and the deeper the value and meaning to you, the greater the chance you have to succeed.

What is Your Purpose in Life?

A good question to ask yourself is, "What is my purpose in life?" I never really knew what my purpose was when I was younger. I just took what life gave me. Yes, I wanted to have a good job and make money. I wanted my family to be secure and happy. I wanted to travel and see as much of the world as possible, but I was never fully focused on a deep purpose to fulfill what I was capable of doing. I was very lucky when I started Productivity Inc. to find so many great geniuses in Japan and bring their amazing knowledge to the West.

I now am very lucky to have found my new purpose in life. **It is for me to be best teacher teaching teachers and managers how to teach students and employees how to be successful in life.** I want to be the best teacher of the Harada Method possible.

Harada Speaking about Purpose

When I first started coaching Track and Field, I was devoted to having my students become No. 1 in Japan in their events. That was my sole goal and purpose. Now when I look back at those days, I see that in a sense I was really selfish. I was looking primarily at how the students' success benefited me. I was not thinking deeply enough about what it meant to the students. The real breakthrough happened when I started to ask to myself, I want them to be number one, but what for? Is it for my students, for their families, to help the students with economic problems, to improve the tough situation at my school, or to cheer up the local community? I then thought differently.

When I was younger, all I could see was myself. Now, I can see myself and other things around me: circumstances, people around me, and the good affect that my work has on others.

A sense of purpose strengthens you and when difficulties come, you can more easily overcome them as you come closer and closer to your goals. Purpose nourishes a sense of mission. It makes the joy of achieving goals much bigger.

Unfortunately, it seems that most people only care about working to make money or to improve their social status. It is time to turn away from this obsession with only profits, and start making the right decisions by following a sense of right and wrong. People should act based on what they think is right. They should avoid doing certain things because they know it is wrong to do them.

Certainly, moral judgments are hard to make—they depend on timing and circumstances, even ones religious beliefs. But they need to be made. In the case of the subprime lending crisis, there would have been a different outcome if bank managers had decided not to sell the risky financial products. Management should have been more concerned about society's well being.

I am very concerned about people's tendency to enrich themselves without a sense of what is right or wrong. Reliable people must have a strong sense of morality, not just the skills or knowledge needed to create economic gains.

The Harada Method has proven to be very effective in guiding people to make correct decisions. It brings a sense of right and wrong to people and companies when many of them were only concerned about making money and demonstrating their own importance. Pursuing prosperity that benefits everyone is more important than pursuing prosperity that only benefits only ourselves. Building work skills is very important but developing a great character should come first.

Of course, profits are very important. Without them, companies could not exist. However, since we are part of this same planet and should be concerned about our mutual wellbeing, morality is a key. Sure there are people that steal, and cheat others for their personal gain, but success is available to everyone without doing dishonest or dishonorable things.

Self-reliant people pursue benefits for others as well as for themselves. Achieving your goals creates both practical and emotional benefits for you and others. There is a proverb that says, "A soul alone neither sings nor weeps." Someone always helps you achieve your goals, regardless of whether you notice them or not. When you realize that someone is always ready to support you, you feel a strong sense of mission and responsibility to keep working. This feeling keeps you continually moving forward and it enhances a sense of pride in you for what you are doing.

I have been interested in sumo wrestling ever since I started visiting Japan over 30 years ago. I receive the sumo matches over cable six times a year. In May of 2012, sumo wrestler Kyokutenho won the "basho," tournament. He fought 15 matches with 40 other wrestlers over 15 days. On the final day, six sumo wrestlers had a chance to win. Kyokutenho was one of the oldest wrestlers, at 38 years old, and had never won an event. He weighed around 347 pounds and his career record was 802 wins and 784 losses - just average. Well this time he won - the oldest wrestler to win in over 87 years. I watched him cry with joy after he won. During the TV interview he said, "I had to do it for the people that supported me." I have seen him fight many times, and I was not at all impressed with his ability, but my whole attitude changed about him when I saw how the spirit moved him and how happy I was for the underachiever who was able to break through and win. It follows Harada's saying - "You never give up."

I like to watch professional football games. I have been a New York Giant fan since I was five years old. Watching the preseason games I saw that the stands were virtually empty but when the season starts it is almost impossible to buy a ticket. The preseason games don't mean anything towards getting to the Super Bowl. It has very little meaning for the football fan. Even when we watch a regular season game, if the score is lopsided many people will leave early and go home. We lose our interest in things when they have little meaning for us. We all want "meaning" in the things we do! Having a strong goal with strong purposes and values gives us meaning, a clear focus, and can keep us highly motivated to succeed in life.

Chapter 8 - Analyze Yourself

"No matter how deep a study you make, what you really have to rely on is your own intuition, and when it comes down to it, you really don't know what's going to happen until you do it."
- Konosuke Matsushita

Analyzing Successes and Failures

Harada stated earlier, to succeed you want to balance the four aspects of yourself: Mental, Skills, Health and Living. Here, in this chapter, you will learn how to analyze and look at your strengths and weaknesses. You want to re-enforce and repeat your strengths, your past successes, and to find ways not to repeat your weaknesses, your past failures. You also want to look at those underlying problems that prevent you from attaining your goals and to find solutions to those problems.

Some people always produce great results and are looked at as talented professionals in their chosen field. Others repeatedly make mistakes and end up not ever succeeding in their careers. What is the difference between these two kinds of people?

The answer is quite simple. Professionals who always get the best results have good habits and the others do not. Fortunately, you can teach yourself to develop new, positive habits.

Attributes of Successful People

One example of an attribute that all successful people share is a high level of self-control or discipline. Self-control is necessary to maintain your efforts in the face of adversity. Self-control allows you to put aside unnecessary distractions and focus on what is important.

Being optimistic is another attribute of successful people. Successful people believe they are in control of their lives, and that they can make their futures better through their own efforts.

The first step of developing attributes such as self-control and optimism is to be aware of the habits you already have. You want to be aware of what has caused you to succeed in the past, so that you will be likely to repeat these behaviors in the future. Likewise, you want to know what caused you to fail in the past so that you can avoid repeating these behaviors.

Learn from Your Past Using the Four Aspects

To help you analyze yourself more thoroughly, as Mr. Harada discovered, you want to look at four areas of your life: **mental**, **skills**, **health** and **life**:

- ∞ **Mental**- focus, confidence, overall attitude
- ∞ **Skills** - knowledge and capabilities - what you can do
- ∞ **Health** - how your body feels, diet, exercise, physical energy, etc.
- ∞ **Life** - relationships with others, work/life balance

Look at Your Past Successes

Look at your past and recall those things you did very well, that you are proud of. You want to be able to repeat your successes over and over again. You want to build on your past success.

Here are some examples of successes from my life:

Mental - I published Dr. Shingo's "A Revolution in Manufacturing - the SMED System." I don't like to gamble because I hate to lose, but I invested heavily in producing this book and it sold over 100,000 copies.

Skills - It took me two years to learn how to publish books, and I made dozens of mistakes, but from 'Not giving up" I was able to publish over 250 management books. My teachers told me I couldn't write; for many years I believed them, and this is my seventh book

Health - To maintain my health, I exercise every single day: 30 minutes on the treadmill and 30 minutes doing yoga and stretching my muscles. It wasn't easy at first. I had a lot of resistance to do it, but now it is a routine that I look forward to.

Living - I meditate every morning. I wash the dishes at night, and I teach at Portland State University, where I am thrilled to see the students applying the Harada Method successfully.

A good exercise is to write down 50 things about yourself that you like, include all the things you were successful with in your past. Then look at the good things from your past and think about how you will repeat them.

I received an email recently from a former student that said, "I took your Japanese Management class a couple of springs ago and graduated last summer. I've been having a frustrating go of it over the past year and haven't been able to crack the job market. I really enjoyed the class, and remember you talking about looking at our resumes. I was wondering if you could take a look at my resume."

I did look at his resume, and saw why he couldn't find a job. The resume showed very few of his positive attributes. It was too short; everything was only on one page. How can you describe twenty or more years about yourself on only one page? There was nothing on the resume that showed what an appealing person he was.

I told him that he needed to redo his entire resume; I suggested instead of just one page write at least a four-page resume filled with many of the 50 things he liked about his past. He needed to tell in more detail his work experience and how well he works in teams, whom he worked for, what he did and how successful the projects were.

I then suggested that his objective statement should be clearer and in more detail telling his central goal, highlighting his strengths: what would he add to a company if they hired him and what does he want to do in the company. I like to read interesting stories and shouldn't a resume be your interesting story telling why you would be invaluable to your new employer?

Then Analyze Your Past Failures

Looking at the same four categories: Mental, Skills Health and Living write down those things in the past where you were not successful, where you made mistakes that you do not want to repeat.

Why Did You Succeed or Fail?

Once you have a list of successes and failures, you want to analyze what caused them. Write down why you believe you were successful or didn't succeed.

Here are a few of my recent successes and failures:

Successes:

Mental - I had a strong will to win. I continue to study almost every night about the Harada Method.

Skills - I followed my 'To Do' list and accomplished everything for the past month. I write around three to four hours almost every day.

Health - I exercise daily. I religiously take my medicine and vitamins.

Living - I did not argue with my wife. I realize that the best way to not argue was to realize that she is always right.

Failures:

Mental - I felt a lot of pressure. I did not keep to my schedule.

Skills - I worked without planning. I missed a few days on writing my book.

Health - I did not sleep enough. I ate the wrong foods.

Living - I took my work stress out on my wife. This is deadly and not something to be repeated.

A Few Examples of Past Successes and Failures

Mental	Positive thinking – relaxed – enjoyed what I do	Complaining – irritated – felt a lot of pressure
Skills	Followed my to do lists – reported, communicated and got some advise – planned in detail	Worked without taking notes – reported only after the incidents occurred – worked without planning
Health	I ate well three times a day – I slept 8 hours a day – I walk three times a week	I went out eating many times – I drank instant coffee too much – I did not enough sleep
Living	My room was clean – I had time to talk to children – I did not argue with my wife	My room is messy – I have no time to talk to my children – I took my work stress out on my wife

Go to the Long-term Goal Setting sheet and write down your past successes and failures with the view that you want to repeat your successes and find ways to avoid making the same mistakes again.

Predict Future Obstacles and Come up with Solutions

After you analyze your past, the next step is to predict what obstacles might lie ahead in your future then write down ways to overcome those obstacles. Again, you want to take a balanced approach, so you need to categorize the obstacles using the four aspects (mental, skills, health and personal life).

Looking at Problems and Solutions

	Underlying problems	Solutions
Mental	I speak negative words - I easily get irritated with troubles - I become nervous	I calm my heart by writing - Be confident as the store manager - List up what needs to be done and organize my work
Skills	I make careless mistakes - I take too much time to deal with emails - I can't handle more than two projects at a time	Do double checks - Decide the timeframe for emails - Manage folders and make to-do-lists
Health	I eat instant foods too many times - Lack of sleep - Backache due to lack of exercises	I ask my wife to make lunch sandwiches - I go to bed before midnight - Take fifteen minutes to stretch in the morning and night
Living	I do not clean my room - I become lazy after coming back from work - I do not take time with my children	I clean my room in the morning during the weekends - I write my journal and stay on top of my priorities -

While you complete this entire self-analysis exercise, dig deep into yourself to find what patterns or traits you have that will stand in the way of your success. Be honest about both your successes and failures. If you take full responsibility for your actions in the past, you are more likely to change your behaviors going forward.

Chapter 9 - Create Your Open Window 64-Chart with Eight Areas to Achieve Your Goals

"Success comes from knowing that you did your best to become the best that you are capable of becoming." - John Wooden

After you complete your self-analysis and have decided on what your main goal will be, you then want to create an action plan for reaching your goal. Creating the Open Window 64-Chart is a key step toward developing your plan. The Open Window 64-Chart is a list of 64 specific actions that you will need to take in the future in order to achieve your goals.

1	2	3
4	Goal	5
6	7	8

To create your chart, you first write your main goal in the center box. For example, as I mentioned before, my goal is to be the best Harada Method teacher in the West.

> To be the best Harada Method teacher in the West

Next, write down eight areas that will help you to reach your goal. The areas should be broad (non-specific) categories. The areas are where you will concentrate your efforts to expand your skills and experiences that will help you to accomplish your goal. For example, I have:

1. Build Skills
2. Marketing
3. Develop Courses
4. Research
5. Health
6. Community
7. Spirit
8. Write

Let's take a look at how Mr. Tahara, from Mr. Harada's example, built his Open Window 64-Chart. First, he wrote down his goal of selling $250,000 worth of products in April. Then he came up with eight areas he needed to work on to reach his goal. Notice how general the eight areas are. They leave plenty of flexibility for coming up with eight tasks for each one.

1. Q=Products	2. S=Service	3. C=Cleanliness
4. Raise the number of customers	Goal: Sell $250,000 of products in April	5. Increase spending per customer
6. Standby	7. Training	8. Manager

One of my students at Portland State University came up with:

1. Skills enhancement
2. Family
3. Mentor
4. Strategic Planning
5. Continuous goal setting
6. Transitioning
7. Leadership
8. Networking

The eight areas that you list will be where you will need to focus your energies on in the future.

Case Study - Alpha Studio, Inc.

Alpha Studio is an educational company, running cram[26] schools, English language schools, and computer schools in Japan. In 2005, Ms. Midori Matsuoka, president of Alpha Studio, came to a Harada Method workshop in Tokyo. Before then, she studied the Harada Method on her own by reading Harada's books and listening to his recorded speeches.

At the workshop, she met Mr. Harada and was struck by his charismatic personality and his true passion for making people self-reliant. In 2006, she decided to bring the Harada Method to her company, with the hope of attaining great results.

Harada had each employee focus at Alpha Studio focus on setting clear goals for themself. In order to make what needed to be done clear to all, and to keep everyone motivated, employees were asked to write down 31 actions to be completed - one for each day of the month.

Employees posted their monthly goal sheets on the wall so that everyone in the office could see them. If something was left unfinished, everyone in the office knew who had not finished their tasks for the day.

---

[26] Cram schools are special private schools that offer lessons conducted after regular school hours and on the weekends.

Ms. Matsuoka also used the Open Window 64-Chart (OW64) to improve company meetings. When she noticed that employees were not giving practical and concrete ideas during a meeting, she stopped the meeting immediately and had her employees think deeper and clearer by writing an Open Window 64-Chart. **The quality of the discussion during each meeting got much better when they used the OW64 system as a group.**

As Ms. Matsuoka hoped the Harada Method worked well for Alpha Studios. One year later, the company's profits showed a year-on-year increase of 200%. **Ms. Matsuoka believed that the key for this big change was to set detailed, time-framed actions for each person.** When employees did this, the company's culture improved dramatically. Employees learned to do something positive no matter what, which translated into much-improved overall results.

Chapter 10 - Write Eight Tasks for Each Area

"Only a life lived for others is worth living." - Albert Einstein

Improve PowerPoint slides by 9/21	Deliver keynotes	Practice Q&E with local companies	Emails to past attendees lists	Develop website	Promote Harada workshops Aug 12-31	Perfect the keynote address	The Harada 5-day certification course Oct. 1	The 3-day course
Do videos Jan 15	**Build Skills**	Work on website	Create an email promotional piece for workshops	**Marketing**	Promote books September 10th	Produce webinar	**Develop courses**	The two-day course
Improve presentation skills	Learn to use pages 8-15	Learn Japanese Jan. 1	Articles - news release once/week	Collect email addresses	Get keynotes	Respect for People	Senior management presentation 9-27	Q&E certification
Study all of Harada's material daily	Read Covey and other success writers	Prepare for daily diary publication Aug 15 2012	**To be the best Harada Method teacher in the West**			Exercise twice a day	Meditate twice a day	Improve my posture
Study innovation	Study and Research	Master System Oct. 15				Set up a precise diet	**Health and Mind**	Shizeng twice a month (1st and 15th)
Study MAP	Integrate Q&E Kaizen to Harada Sept. 15	Learn Adobe software				Carefully monitor my blood pressure	Drink 6 glasses of water a day	Shake off tensions
Teach at PSU Sept. 27	Teach Harada to other teachers Jan 1	Work at a local charity Dec. 15	Meditate twice a day	Friday with Alfred	Imagine what is possible	Story book - start Jan. 1	Write the Harada book every day - complete by 12/31	The training manual - complete by October 1st
Do the dishes and keep house clean daily	**Community and Family**	Do 55 - remove books Sept. 1	Stop wandering thoughts	**Spirit**	Summarize Ponlon, Kukai and Inamori	To major management media - every other week	**Write**	Write monthly newsletter 1st of month
Help students with their resumes and interviews at class	Speak to local groups	Noriko accounting 8-14	Observe - listen - Stop daily for a few minutes	Read spiritual works - daily	Inside when speaking - work on this	To senior leaders two per week	Daily diary every day	CEO newsletter Nov. 1

After you have picked eight areas to focus on, you next will then write eight specific actions or tasks within each area (8 areas x 8 actions = 64). For example, in each of the boxes surrounding **Study and Research**, I wrote the following tasks:

1. Study all of Harada's material

2. Read Stephen Covey and other motivational writers

3. Prepare for Diary publication

4. Learn Adobe software

5. Study innovation

6. Integrate Quick and Easy Kaizen with Harada

7. Study the Production Technology MAP

8. Master the Harada system

Repeat this process for each of the remaining areas to complete your 64-Chart.

Your goal is to write eight tasks within each area. For some areas, you might have more than eight tasks. In other areas, you will struggle to come up with the eight tasks. If this is the case, you might need to revise the area as it may be too specific.

Mr. Harada says you should be able to list the 64 tasks in 32 minutes. This will force you to think vigorously.

In the Harada Method, there are two kinds of actions: one is time-based actions, or **tasks**, and the other is **routines**. Tasks are actions that have expected completion dates. Routines are actions you do on a recurring basis. When you created your Open Window 64-Chart, some of the actions you wrote down were tasks and some were routines. You will use the two types in different ways.

Listed below is an example of eight specific actions around one area:

Perfect the keynote address	The Harada 5-day certification course Oct. 1	The 3-day course
Produce webinar	**Develop courses**	The two-day course
Respect for People	Senior management presentation 9-27	Q&E certification

If your goal is to "accomplish $160,000 sales by December 1, 2012," one of your tasks might be, "I will make a detailed plan for sales promotion activities by July 1." Another task could be, "I will prepare 40,000 flyers for distribution by May 15th."

You should be careful when you pick your tasks because they need to be directly linked to achieving your goal. As you select them, ask yourself "Is this really useful? Is this something that moves me closer to my goal?" You will never be able to get what you want if you keep doing things that are not directly linked to your goal.

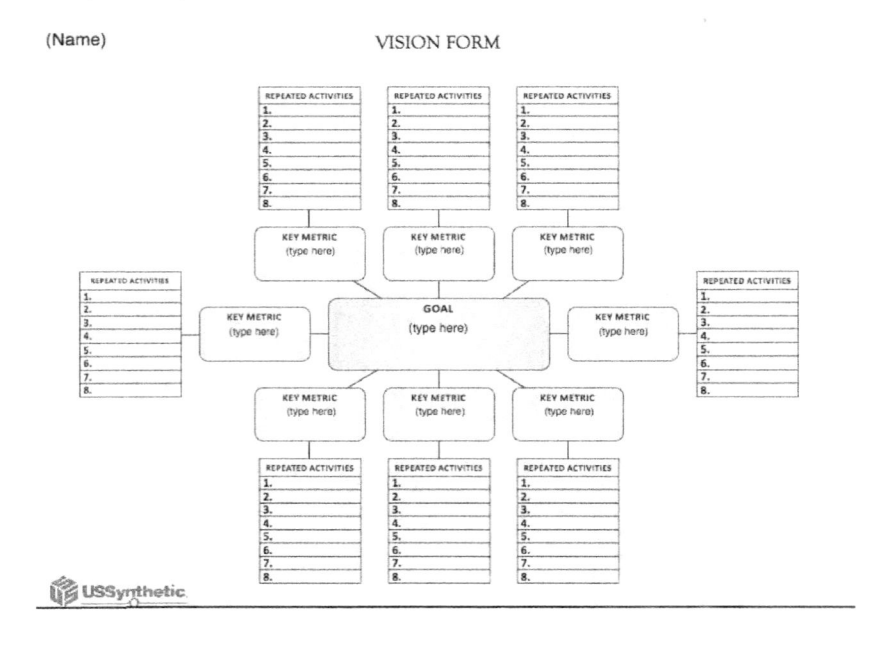

(Name)   VISION FORM

[Vision Form diagram with central GOAL surrounded by eight KEY METRIC boxes, each linked to a list of REPEATED ACTIVITIES (1-8). USSynthetic logo at bottom left.]

Hema Heimuli a training manager at US Synthetics in Utah and one of my workshop students created a wonderful variation of the 64-chart.

Chapter 11 - Write a Start Date for Each Task

"The Toyota style is not to create results by working hard. It is a system that says there is no limit to people's creativity.

People don't go to Toyota to 'work' they go there to 'think.'"
- Taiichi Ohno, former Vice President Toyota

Add Due Dates

Sixty-four tasks are more than you can accomplish at one time, so you will have to prioritize which ones to do first. After completing the 64-Chart, go back and put start or end dates on as many of the tasks as you can. This will help you to select the first top ten tasks you want to start with first.

Emails to past attendees lists	Develop website	Promote Harada workshops Aug 12-31
Create an email promotional piece for workshops	Marketing	Promote books September 10th
Articles - news release once/week	Collect email addresses	Get keynotes

Chapter 12 - Select 10 Tasks to Get Started

"Perceiving and thinking are not the same. Perceiving uses the five senses. Thinking is our mental ability to pursue cause and purpose by objectively asking 'why' about all phenomena."
- Dr. Shigeo Shingo

Go over your 64-Chart and select ten tasks based on start date, those that you want to start doing right away to attain your goal. Include the date when you want to start.

Mr. Tahara's example:

By When	Tasks from your 64 chart in order of occurrence
By 4/4	I will review the monthly plan on how to foster sales
By 4/5	I will research the number of customers who visited us last month
By 4/7	I will mail out 3,000 direct mails
By 4/10	I will visit 20 different companies for sales negotiation
By 4/13	I will call for some classified ads
By 4/14	I will review the monthly plan and revise it if necessary
By 4/15	I will conduct the mid-term inventory-check
By 4/20	I will calculate the sales estimate
By 4/21	I will calculate the store revenue estimate
By 4/24	I will estate the F/L

You will use this list on your Daily Diary, which we will discuss soon. You will select a few tasks from this list on what you want to do each day to attain your goal. Once you accomplished your tasks, you then go back to this list and take another task to place on to your Daily Dairy. You should at least once a month redo the above list and take new tasks from your 64-Chart that you want to do this month.

Chapter 13 - Build New Habits With New Routines

"Leadership, like coaching, is fighting for the hearts and souls of men and getting them to believe in you." - Eddie Robinson, Former Football Coach, Grambling State University

Most of us follow patterns, habits, and routines without being conscious if those routines are helping us or not. We eat too much; we drink too much; we talk too much; we don't exercise enough, etc.

If you want to achieve your goals, you have to break those old habits that are destructive to you. The best way to do this is to establish new, positive routines. Routines are a series of actions that you will do on a daily or weekly basis to build new patterns in your life.

When I was young, I smoked three packs a day. Miraculously, when I was 35 I was able to give up smoking, even though it took me two years to do it. When I finally gave up smoking cigarettes, I replaced smoking with eating more food and gained 25 pounds very quickly. I tell people if they want to give up smoking "cold turkey" it is very hard unless you can find a substitute. Every time I got an urge for a cigarette I should have drunk a glass of water instead of eating something. I would not have gained so much weight and my kidneys would have been much happier.

You want to change your old habits to new ones, but you don't want to pick up a habit that is harmful. This can be done properly. Every successful person at some point in their life realized the importance of following new routines to attain their goals. Following the Harada Method you will start to replace your old routines with positive new ones that will help you attain your goals.

How to Pick Your Routines

The routines you choose can come from various sources. You can choose them from your 64-Chart. You can go back and look at your 33 words and select from the actions you want to take to become fully self-reliant. You can also look at the analysis section of your Long-Term Goal setting sheet and use the things in your past you did to be successful. Also, look at what caused your past failures and write out new routines to avoid repeating those failures.

Routine actions in the order of importance
I will review my action by journaling
I will take notes of what can be improved at the end of the day and work better tomorrow
Increase the revenue by checking the F/L
I will praise my employees each day
I will distribute 100 flyers to passerby's
I will do simulation to achieve the sales goals of the day
I will stretch for thirty minutes after taking a bath
I will read my credo before starting to work to prepare my heart
I will exchange my journal with my children and communicate more with my family
I will check the sales and revenue and modify the term goals on the report

It is not easy to change patterns. We are creatures of habit. In all my college classes students will pick a seat to sit, and if I did not say anything they would sit in the exact same seat each week.

Mr. Harada tells us to pick a new routine and, if possible, to do it for 1000 days - then you might trust yourself to repeat that new pattern and not go back to your old way of doing things.

Some routines you will do daily and some maybe once or twice a week. Since this is your goal and your life plan, you decide what needs to be done and when. Always keep your goal in mind and take things day by day, so you don't become frustrated and stop trying to change.

You can take a little survey and write down all of the routines you do in day over and over again, some for your benefit and some not for your benefit. Try it.

Taiichi Ohno would draw a circle[27] on the floor in the middle of the factory and ask senior managers, especially those with Toyota suppliers, to stand in the circle for the entire day and just observe what goes on in the plant. At the end of the day he would return and ask the manager what she observed. He wanted you to see all of the waste that was happening in the factory. This is a very simple but powerful process to teach a lesson to senior managers. I recommend you do the same thing. Just stand and watch people for an entire day and

---

[27] Go to the Jeffrey Liker interview in the back of the book to read more about Ohno's circle.

observe the wastes and the unproductive routines being done.

Case Study - J Com

Mr. Okuda, the former executive secretary of Cosmo Securities, left the company in 2008 and soon joined Jupiter Telecommunications (J Com).

After joining J Com, he took many on-the-job training courses to learn more about sales and marketing. Most people might take years to learn about sales and marketing, but Mr. Okuda wanted to learn fast so he finished the training courses in six months.

After working as a sales manager at two branches, he was assigned as the bureau chief of the Hokusetsu Branch in February 2009.

The Hokusetsu Branch was the worst in sales of all 52 branches in the company. In the two years prior to Mr. Okuda's arrival, the Hokusetsu Branch was not able to achieve its expected sales targets.

To turn the branch around, the first thing Okuda did was to explain his management philosophy to the employees. He also had a short interview with each of them to find out what they were thinking and what they really wanted to achieve.

Mr. Okuda wanted the employees to build their own positive habits to produce better results. He taught the employees techniques from his own experience that he knew were useful for increasing sales. He then let employees set their own routine actions.

Mr. Okuda let the employees set not only results-directed actions, but also character-directed actions such as cleaning up or doing volunteer work. . They used the Harada Routine Check Sheet to monitor how well they completed their daily tasks.

Mr. Okuda believed that J Com salespeople must look and be happy, because what they sell - cable television, Internet and cell phone service - is very important to the daily lives of customers. **Mr. Okuda said that a good salesperson that sells things has to have a certain aura of happiness. He says that everyday routines and smiling faces can provide that atmosphere.**

To make the workplace more energetic and motivating, Mr. Okuda posted each employee's goals and phrases to inspire them on the walls of the office.

In May 2009, the Hokusetsu Branch achieved its sales goals for the first time in two years. In August 2009, his branch became No. 1 out of all the 52 branches in getting contracts from new customers. The branch got many awards for its outstanding results.

While proud of the branch's improvement, Mr. Okuda could see that uncertainties still lay ahead for J Com. The Japanese Broadcasting System was changing from analogue to digital that summer. Mr. Okuda thought the changes would benefit the company, but he was not 100% sure. **However, he was confident that the company's focus on employee development would help it compete going forward.**

"If you want to succeed," he said, "do what is

right, and let your employees do what is right. Be positive, aggressive, and keep smiles on your faces.

Chapter 14 - Write Affirmations (Self-Talk)

"We make people untrustworthy by not showing them enough trust"
- Kaoru Ishikawa, father of Quality Control Circles

At some point, while you pursue your goal you will run into resistance from yourself, from others or from your circumstances. One of the most dangerous forms of resistance is that voice in your head that says you aren't good enough to succeed. To counteract this negativity, use **affirmations**.

Affirmations are statements that will keep your energy very positive as you work towards achieving your goal. Last year, I was watching the New York Knicks playing the Dallas Mavericks on television. Thanks to the outstanding performance of Jeremy Lin, the Knicks won. Throughout the game, you could watch the players shout encouragement to each other. They huddled and cheered themselves on to make themselves believe they could win. When they believed they could win, they did.

Affirmations can give you a completely new mindset. I like to say "I am better and better in every way, every day."

To me affirmations are also a form of chanting, repeating over and over again words to inspire you to change your behavior. When I was younger, I was afraid of flying. Every time the plane took off or landed, I would literally shake with fear. I didn't know what to do. My job required me to travel, but I dreaded it. Once I took a boat from Europe to America just to avoid flying. Another time, I had five martinis before getting on the plane to Paris, and I am not a drinker and the martinis didn't help at all.

A special type of affirmation rescued me from my fears. Somehow, I learned about a Hindu "mantra" (song) and started to chant it. I wasn't a Hindu, but I was willing to try anything to get rid of my fear of flying. I chanted to myself every spare moment for one month and miraculously - I don't know exactly how it happened - but all of my fears disappeared. The fear of flying, the fear of heights, the fear of the dark, and the fear to trying new things - they no longer bothered me. Intellectually, I still do not understand how chanting some foreign words could make my fears disappear but I am very grateful. Somehow the vibration that came from my chanting was able to change my behavior.

Here's another way to use affirmations. If you are anything like me, sometimes you wake up in the morning and feel lazy and depressed. You don't know why you feel that way but you do. And believe me, if you feel lousy you will surely spread it to others. But you have a choice. You can accept your negative feelings and have a bad day or you can repeat a positive affirmation over and over and change your state of mind.

You can become your own cheerleader and shout out words that continually encourage you to do well. If it works at sporting events, it will work for you. So think of positive phrases to become your own cheerleader.

My first Harada training was to be given to senior managers at Suncor Corporation in Canada. I did prepare thoroughly but since it was going to be my first, I was nervous, very unusual for me, but I did feel insecure. Well, I believed in Mr. Harada's method, so before the event I repeated over and over again to myself. "Look Norman, you will be great!" And I do believe my presentation went over very well.

Often, people repeat negative statements in their minds without even being aware of what they are doing. Do you keep thinking and telling yourself that you cannot do something, that you are too lazy, that you lack inner strength, or that you are going to fail? Your subconscious mind accepts as true what you keep saying, so why not choose only positive statements?

Repeating positive statements to yourself over and over again somehow helps you change your behavior. It is used in all sports. Almost every religion uses the repetition of words to help change behaviors. Continually repeating affirmations with conviction and passion will chip away at even the strongest resistance inside of you.

Use Sayings to Encourage Yourself and Others

Many leaders in Japan come up with sayings. These are words that inspire people to rise to their greatness. For example, I like the Lexus motto of "The passionate pursuit of perfection." It is a wonderful phrase to motivate people to continuously improve. I also like what a past chairman at Toyota said, "I want Toyota to build a new car that can drive from New York to Los

Angeles on one tank of gasoline." What an amazing vision to inspire the creative genius from so many of Toyota's workers. That is what great leaders do - they inspire their followers.

Imagine that you are swimming with your friends in a swimming pool. They swim fifteen laps - something you have never done before. You want to win their respect by showing them that you can make it too. You start swimming, and at the same time keep repeating in your mind, "I can do it. I can do it..." You keep thinking and believing that you are going to complete the fifteen laps. What are you actually doing? You are repeating positive affirmations. Eventually, your mind will believe what you tell it and you will be able to finish. When you repeat your affirmations with attention, conviction, interest and desire, you can, as the saying goes, "move mountains."

Chapter 15 - Determine What Kind of Support You Need

*"It is not necessary to change.
Survival is not mandatory."*

*"It is not enough to do your best.
You must know what to do, and then
do your best."* - W. Edwards Deming

What kind of support do you need to attain your goal? Everyone needs help from time to time. Every great athlete, for example, needs a coach. Gabby Douglas won two gold medals in gymnastics in the last Olympics, and always worked with a coach to help her improve her performance or to observe her body movement and give her feedback. If the greatest athletes need a coach, you should realize you need one and find someone to help you attain your goal.

Some people can do it alone, but it is very hard to step back and know exactly what your needs are. There are some things you cannot do by yourself at any cost, even if they are important and absolutely necessary to achieve your goal. When you run into obstacles like this, instead of giving up ask someone to help you.

Almost all successful people are good at helping and being helped. Think hard about what kind of help you will need to attain your goal. Ask yourself questions such as, "What are my weaknesses?" and "What do I need to learn to accomplish my goal?"

In the example below, Mr. Tahara says he needs the following types of support:

"Follow up with the sales outcome."

"Assisting in staffing during the weekends."

"Report the accurate information."

Another example:

| Contents of support for achieving goals | Support and advice, Sharing the passion, goal, and vision, Emotional support, report about the part-timers |

Clarify the Support You Need

Successful professionals prepare thoroughly for the future. They know in advance how they want to be helped, and they regularly communicate with certain people who give them guidance. They create an environment that makes it easier for them to achieve their goals.

Writing has always been a challenge for me. I did not learn as a child sentence structure and grammar, I would also be totally lost without the computer's spell checkers. With each book, this is the seventh for me written in these past ten years I have had at least two or three people edit the text before publishing.

I also need help on my web site, promoting my books and many other aspects of my business. I am very grateful of the support I get.

Case Study - ANA Communications Co., Ltd.

Mr. Wada is a manager of the Operation Management Department at ANA Communications and a certified Harada Method training coach.

After Lehman's fall in 2009, ANA Communications established a task force for productivity enhancement. One of the tools chosen to enhance productivity was the Harada Diary. In July 2010, the Harada Diary was introduced to the operation management department. In 2011, the department's productivity increased 50%.

Ms. Sai, an employee in the operations management department, said the Harada Diary made a big difference for her.

"At first, I thought writing the Harada Diary every day was nothing but a bother," she said. "I wondered why I had to do such a thing outside my daily work. I was already very busy. But as I reluctantly kept writing it, I started to realize that the diary was absolutely necessary for making positive changes. By writing the Harada Diary, I can figure out important business matters and give myself a positive attitude before working on projects. In addition, the diary is a very useful and effective way to communicate with my boss."

"When I write down what to do each day in the Harada Diary, I feel motivated and make up my mind to complete the day's tasks - no matter what. My boss writes messages in my diary every day, and it helps me a lot to continue writing it. I have kept writing the diary for more than one year because I feel the powerful effects of writing it."

Ms. Sai's boss, Mr. Nishigai, explained the benefits from his perspective.

"The Harada Diary is my day-to-day management tool," he said. "It helps me maintain good communication with my employees. Sometimes, they write something that is hard to say when we talk face-to-face."

According to Mr. Nishigai, the improved communication is making a big difference at ANA. "Bosses gauge how well their employees are doing with their tasks by reading their diaries," he said. "The Harada Diary allows us to take quick and decisive measures when we notice delays in our employees' projects. The diary has been instrumental in increasing our organization's productivity.

Chapter 16 - Select People to Support You

"What makes a good coach? Complete dedication."
- George Halas, former coach of Chicago Bears football team. In 40 years as a coach, he endured only six losing seasons.

No one can achieve everything they want to by themselves: No one. Therefore, you need to develop a support system if you want to be successful.

I was watching the Olympic swimming team trials and after each event the reporter would interview the winner. Many of the athletes immediately praised and thanked their coach for their support. It was as if it was a team effort, even though only one person did the swimming.

The first step is for you too to find a coach, someone with experience who can help guide you forward to succeed and win. You need someone who will encourage you when you are discouraged; someone who will keep you accountable for your actions (or lack thereof). A coach will help you stay motivated and sustain your efforts. Choosing the right coach will make a tremendous difference as you work toward your goal.

Your coach should be someone you trust to have your best interests in mind. He or she will review your

Harada Method forms to see if you have been completing them, and give you feedback on a daily, weekly or monthly basis - in order to make sure you are on staying on the right path.

The best coach will be someone who has more experience than you do, an experienced manager, for example, but sometimes you might work with someone who is at the same level as yourself. Who do you know that wants you to succeed and is also willing to be honest with you?

In addition to having a good coach, you also want to have a network of people who will be willing to help you when you need it. Think about who would want to support you? It could be a spouse, a manager, a colleague or a friend. You could also ask more than one person to help you.

Mr. Tahara's example:

Supporters for achieving goals	Mr. Tanaka the associate manager, Mr. Moriyana the area manager

Harada's Experience on Becoming a Coach

It will be helpful to show you how I developed my ideas to grow people by looking back at my experiences as a track and field athlete.

I joined the track and field club at my junior high school when I entered the 7th grade. I was trying to follow the same path my older brother had taken. In fact, I joined the club because I really respected my brother, who was also team captain. Although I was an athletic-minded child, I was only an ordinary runner.

My brother, on the other hand, was a superstar athlete who made it to the national championships many times in both high school and college. I had a much less successful career, and I only barely made it to the local championship once when I was a college student. For me, participating in an athletic competition at the national level was a pipe dream.

Still, I was a very enthusiastic athlete. In junior high, I never missed practice - not even one day. I was a middle-distance runner, running the 400-meter dash, the 800-meter run and the 400-meter hurdles. My success did not match my enthusiasm, but I really liked my coach, my teammates and the variety of club activities.

One day when I was in the 9th grade, my coach asked me if I wanted to be the team captain. I was bewildered by his question. I did not think I was cut out for it, unlike my brother the superstar athlete. I asked my coach "Do you really mean it? I don't think I deserve it because I am not a great runner."

He answered, **"It doesn't matter if the captain is a great athlete. What matters is that the person has an ability to lead and manage people.**[28] Takashi, you have that ability and I want you to be the captain."

---

[28] The Yale University swimming and diving coach Bob Kiphuth, was a five-time Olympic coach and one of the greatest collegiate coaches ever, amassing an unparalleled dual-meet record of 528-13 in more than 40 years at Yale. He did not even have a college degree.

I pondered what the coach said about me—that I had the ability to lead and manage people. I was not sure if I really had the ability, but I trusted him and decided to take the position. By assuming the captain's role, I realized that I had the strength to lead and manage people effectively. To my great surprise, I was later selected to be captain of all the track and field teams I belonged to throughout high school and college. This demonstrated how good I was at leading and managing people.

Many people have the wrong idea about what it takes to be an excellent coach or leader. They believe that a great coach needs to have a notable athletic record while growing up. They think that having a great record in the past provides enough teaching expertise for people to become great coaches. In fact, every time my students won a gold medal in the championships, people asked me, "Were you also a great athlete when you were young?" Many said, "I bet you have experience competing at a national level. What was your best 800-meter run record?" People automatically assume that an excellent coach used to be a great athlete.

I want to emphasize that a true coach or leader has the skill set to effectively manage people in addition to specific expertise or great experiences to share with their students. On a great track and field team, there is always someone who has very strong management skills to lead people to success. In great companies, too, there is someone at the senior level who can lead others by managing them effectively.

Chapter 17 - Use Your Routine Check Sheet

"The chains of habit are generally too small to be felt until they are too strong to be broken." - Samuel Johnson

Establishing new routines takes real work. Even with the best intentions, it is easy to fall back on old bad habits. As the New Year approaches every year, many of us recognize it as a good time to give up some old habits and to pick up new ones. We make New Year's resolutions with sincere intentions to keep them. Yet shortly thereafter we fall back into our old patterns.

"Habit is habit, and not to be flung out of the window by anyone, but coaxed downstairs a step at a time." - Mark Twain

Mr. Harada recognizes this frailty in human behavior to follow old patterns and has developed his new system to help you keep your new routines and not fall back to your old ways. One of the most powerful Harada Method tools to help you develop new habits is the Routine Check Sheet.

The Routine Check Sheet is a place for you to watch and score your daily accomplishments. You take the routines you wrote down on the Long-Term Goal Form and write them on the Routine Check Sheet. Here every day you will record every day your success in keeping your promises to yourself.

[Routine Check Sheet - blank template]

Every evening, take a few seconds to record which routines you did on the Routine Check Sheet. If you did the routine, place a 1 or X in the box. If you skipped it that day, write a 0. Add up the number of routines you did each day and write this down at the bottom of each column. This will give you a daily score. Recording your score every day will keep you motivated and on track toward building new habits.

[Routine Check Sheet - example for Unix Corporation]

		Activities - Routine	Evaluation								
Service Activity	At Home	When I come back home, I put my shoes neatly side by side	Other family members have started arranging their shoes in the entrance, keeping the house clean		o	o	o	o	o	o	
	At Work	After arriving at work, I clean the windows of the office for 10 minutes	After doing this for a month, three of my staff have started this kind of service activity		o	x	x			o	
	1	I call twenty customers for outbound sales between 9:00am and 10:00am	By September 30, my overall sales increased 10%		x	o	o			o	
	2	I give encouragement to my mentee via email	As a result, my mentee improves his productivity by 15%		o	o	x	o	o	o	

At the end of every month, you should write out a new list of routines to perform during the next month.

Breaking Away from Old Ideas

It is funny the habits we acquire and end up believing that they are positive for us. I remember once I was in Big Indian, New York, working with a group of people who were trying to refurbish an old hotel. Early Saturday morning, I worked with a few other men building a stone wall. Many properties in New England were divided by stone walls held together without the use of cement. If done properly, these walls could stand for centuries. Each stone required two or three men to lift. As we worked, I was super careful and a little suspicious. I was afraid that one of the other men might shirk their responsibility and allow the stone to slide towards me. But I was not harmed and after four hours of working on the wall I felt full of energy and we all stopped for lunch.

"Habits are at first cobwebs, then cables."
- Spanish Proverb

During lunch, instead of just being quiet, I spoke as I ate to another person. As I spoke, I felt the energy inside me start to escape. At the end of lunch, I was very tired and walked over to my teacher, Rudi, and said, "Rudi, I am a little tired from the morning work and I think I should take a short nap before working again."

Rudi said, "Norman, don't take a nap, just go and work on the wall and your energy will all come back in 20 minutes." I thought he was stretching the truth but I did respect him and I listened and went back to work. He turned out to be right - except it didn't take 20 minutes, it only took 10 minutes, and I was able to work another four hours non-stop. The great lessons I learned at that moment were: first, instead of going to sleep to get energy, I could work hard to get rid of being tired. Second, I should always trust Rudi. And thirdly, and I know my wife Noriko would agree, I should be enjoying her meals and be quiet when I eat.

> **"Motivation is what gets you started.
> Habit is what keeps you going."
> - Jim Ryun**

As you establish new routines, you want to test your old beliefs that have confined you to your old patterns. As mentioned earlier, Mr. Harada suggests you pledge to do a new routine for 1000 days, to engrain the new habit so it becomes permanent with you.

A self-reliant person, a so-called "high achiever," is always consciously or subconsciously creating good habits to motivate themselves to perform at their highest level. Over time, the accumulation of good habits will make you very successful.

You Build Your Skills and Capabilities One Step at a Time. The Magic to Success is Perseverance - Always Moving Forward Towards Your Goals and Never Giving Up

Benefits of the Harada Routine Check Sheet

1. You begin to have real control over your way of life.

2. Instead of working blindly, not knowing if you are on the right track, you can work positively and effectively. You see the daily results of your work.

3. You can measure the affect of what you do as you work towards achieving your goals.

4. You build up your character and develop a strong will by continuously working on your routines.

5. You develop a great sense of self-confidence by working on your routines every day and allowing nothing to pull you away from attaining your goals.

6. You see what you do and what you didn't do over the past month by looking at only one sheet of paper.

7. If you are a manager, you can also see how your employees are changing themselves for the better.

Chapter 18 - Keep a Daily Diary

"I do not try to dance better than anyone else. I only try to dance better than myself."
- Mikhail Baryshnikov

The Harada Daily Diary is where you will put everything to schedule your activities, write down the tasks/actions you want to do that day, and monitor yourself to make sure you are doing what you need to do.

Years ago, when I owned a data processing company in New York City, I would wake up in the middle of night remembering something that I should have done the previous day. Of course, once I was awake it was very difficult to go back to sleep. And then one day, I saw my partner preparing his to-do list. He used a long yellow sheet to write down those items he wanted to do and would then follow the list precisely - one at a time. I copied him immediately, and from that day forward I religiously prepared a to-do list every day.

Once I started using the list, I did not have to get up in the middle of the night anymore because all my "to do" items and notes were now written down. It was my "A3,[29]" my personal "Hoshin Planning[30]" system, all on one sheet of paper.

---

[29] A3 is a document (11 X 17 inches) initially started at Toyota as a problem-solving tool to lead all managers to adhere to a leader's vision throughout the organization.

[30] Hoshin, a Japanese word meaning policy ("needle" pointing direction"), Planning - is a method devised to capture and

Today, I use the Harada Daily Dairy, which is considerably more precise than my old to-do lists. By using the diary I can better organize my day. It keeps my schedule, shows me the tasks I want to do to attain my target and is a place for me to jot down new items and keeps me much better organized.

At either the end of the day or the beginning of the next day, I write my Daily Diary. The first line is for the date and Today's Phrase. The phrase is something to remind me to stay focused, to motivate me, to get me passionate about my life and work. For example, "I will work on writing the Harada book today," was on my Daily Diary for a long time, since it took me quite awhile to write this book.

Date			Today's Phrase	
9/4/2011	Better and better every day, stick to the road, you'll arrive one day.			
Time	Plan	Reflections	Top 5 Tasks for Today	
6:00			1. Have lunch with other co-workers	
			2. Learn quickly how to deal with a problem	
7:00	Wake up	6:30 woke up	3. Caution with mistakes in writing	
			4. Remember to sanitize my hands	
8:00			5. Answer loudly	
	8:30 - Clean	Washed and cleaned	Daily notes, future things to do	
9:00			almost out of cleaner - pick some up at store tomorrow	
10:00	Go shopping			
11:00	Leave for work			

Top 5 Tasks for Today
1.
2.
3.
4.
5.

cement strategic goals as well as flashes of insight about the future and develop the means to bring these into reality.

Under the section "Top 5 Tasks for Today," you should write the important things you want to do today and, if possible, take one or two tasks from your Long-Term Form.

Then you plan your day, and write down the things you want to do, including tasks you need to do to work towards your over all goal, then add anything else that needs to be done at work or at home. The Daily Diary is your reminder list.

12:00		
	Lunch	
1:00		
	Meet with Ann	
2:00		
	Write book	
3:00		
4:00	Call Phil	
	Write in Diary	

At the end of the day, you would write your reflections to see if you did what you wanted to do.

Time	Task	Result
12:00	Lunch	Ate
1:00	Meet with Ann	She agreed on the promotional piece
2:00	Write book	Wrote 20 pages
3:00		
4:00	Call Phil	Set up next week's appointment
	Diary	Updated my diary

Daily notes, future things to do

In addition to writing down your schedule of tasks, appointments, phone calls, etc., you should write down new things that happen during the day and future things to do. You can also use the back of the sheet to jot down notes or write new ideas that come to you during the day.

Area	Description	Score	Comments
Overall	Impression of day		Did you achieve your objective?
Mental	Enthusiasm, focus		Did you have the passion and concentration today?
Body	Diet, exercise, etc.		How was your energy level?
Work	Skill improvement		Did you improve today?
Relations	Work with others		How was your relationship with others?
Life	Personal life		Was it a great day?
Learning	Self-study		Did you learn new things?
Routines	Did many or few		What was it like to go through your routines?
Score each 1-5	TOTAL		

At the end of the day, you need to review what you did score yourself on a scale of 1 to 5, and see if you are sticking to what you wanted to do to attain your goals. You can add also a brief comment next to your score.

Challenges and good things noticed today

What would you do differently?

Inspiring words, phrases, events

In addition, you then write down the challenges you met during the day and the positive things that happened.

Then you think about what you could have done differently to maximize your time and effort. And then you should also write down things that inspired you during the day.

Lastly, I write down things to discuss with your coach or mentor. It would be great if you could meet with your coach for a few minutes each day. After people take my Harada Workshop, I offer to work as their initial coach and have them send me their forms to review.

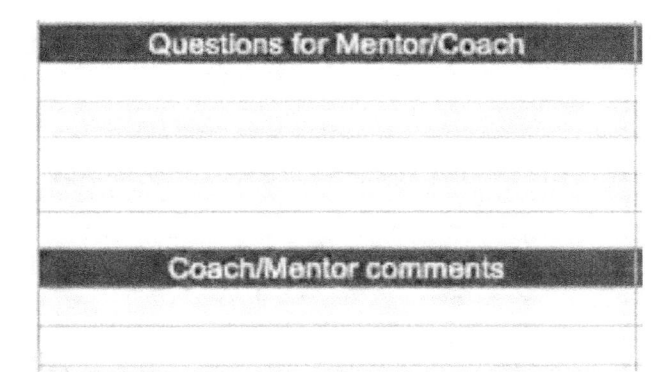

Questions for Mentor/Coach
Coach/Mentor comments

    I attempt to create a Daily Dairy everyday - including weekends. To me, it is my most valuable business tool to accomplish my multiple tasks. I have found it allows me to stay on target and is worth the time it takes each day to complete.

    Using this instrument has allowed me to publish and write new books, run workshops and trainings in many places in the world, teach at both college and at conferences, and to consult with companies. It keeps me organized - not an easy thing to do with my scattered mind.

    My personal Daily Diary, front and back, is covered with notes, which I review at the end of every day or the beginning of the next day to create my new Daily Diary.

Use the Power of Writing

    Harada wants us to "write-write-write" because writing is a very creative process. If you look at the great figures in history, you will find that most of them wrote regularly. Einstein was famous for taking notes. Leonardo da Vinci was prolific with his writing in notebooks with precise illustrations and a vast amount of ideas and inventions. Edison kept his thoughts in 3,000 notebooks. These notebooks enable all of us to understand what these giants thought about when they were alive. What you write indeed shows what you think. Writing stimulates your creative process.

As history illustrates, high performers think and write. We want you to follow their footsteps to ensure your success. We encourage you to make writing in a journal, or diary a daily habit. Make keeping your diary one of your good habits. The Harada Diary is a very useful and powerful tool to organize yourself every day and make sure you stay on target towards your goal.

The Diary as a Tool for Self-Coaching

There is a difference between the words teaching and coaching. Both teaching and coaching require at least two people, you and your teacher, or you and your coach. But the difference is clear. Teaching is a way to lead someone to the optimal solution to their problems. Coaching is a way to help someone bring out the answers from within themself. Teaching adds a lot of knowledge while coaching gets you to experience and apply that knowledge.

For educating beginners and people who tend to be stuck in one pattern, teaching them can be a very effective way to help expand their knowledge and understanding. On the other hand, coaching will help them understand how to use their knowledge and experiences in the most effective way for achieving their success.

As mentioned before, having a coach can be incredibly valuable for helping you to reach your goal, but sometimes you may not have a coach available. It may take time to find your coach, but the Daily Diary can help you stay on track and be, in a way, your own coach. The Diary helps you be your own coach simply by your taking the time to reflect on your day and writing everything down. You can see yourself from an outsider's perspective using the Harada Diary. You just stop and look careful at your daily diary and see what you accomplished and what still has to be done.

Yes, it is better to have someone who you respect to review your diary. When you know that someone else will be looking at the diary, you will put more effort into it. But if that's not possible, your diary will help to keep you on track.

The Powerful Impact of the Harada Diary

There are many ways that the Harada Method helps you toward reaching your goals. These include:

1. Helping you manage your schedule.

2. Preparing you for future success by doing a mental rehearsal, pre-planning your day, and detailing your steps to get there.

3. Prioritizing your "to-do's" - Selecting and focusing on the important things to do.

4. Realizing what you did well and not so well each day - self analysis.

5. Providing drive, energy and courage to enhance your self-confidence.

6. Growing the habit of thinking positively.

7. Developing positive habits that will lead you to success.

8. Recognizing what is needed to achieve goals and purposes.

Managing Your Time Schedule

To increase your own productivity, you want to manage your time efficiently. The Harada Diary helps you do that by giving you a space to write down each day's schedule. By planning your schedule in advance, you can imagine what you will do clearly and precisely. You will wake up and not have to hesitate for a moment about what to do next.

As you prepare your schedule, remember these tips:

9. Write when you plan to arrive / leave your workplace.

10. Write when you plan to take a lunch break.

11. Write what you do in the morning and in the evening in detail.

12. Write when you plan to wake up and go to bed.

13. Write what you plan to do from the time you wake up to the time you arrive at your workplace to make your morning better.

14. Write what you plan to do from the time you leave your workplace to the time you go to bed to make your next day better.

15. Check the most important tasks of the day with a red pen.

16. Write what you plan to do to enhance your job performance taken from your 64 task list.

I can get totally lost in front of my computer. It often will make me feel dizzy, but if I follow my diary precisely, I will take the necessary breaks away from the computer.

Praise and Today's Phrase

On my last visit to Japan, Mr. Harada spoke about his new book on praise. Japanese people are very reluctant to praise themselves. There is an old trite expression about Japan, "The head that pops up gets cut off." Self-praise is scorned upon, inflating your ego, but people do need support. They need positive feedback to keep them motivated. Harada says that if you are not getting enough positive support from others then you have to do it yourself.

In the Diary, under "Today's Phrase," write a saying to encourage yourself, something that increases your enthusiasm and determination. Talk to yourself to keep your spirits high.

Example: "I can do it. I will win."

"I am happy that I finished writing the chapter."

Challenges and Good Things You Noticed Today

One of the functions of the Harada Diary is to help you reflect on your day. Please write as many good things you did during the day as possible. By writing them down, you improve how you feel about yourself.

Remember to add the reasons why you feel you got the results as well. Believing in your own competence on the job motivates you towards improving more.

In addition to writing about what happened at work, write down what you think helped you grow to be a better person. Helping an elderly person cross the street or joining a voluntary cleanup activity are good examples.

You should also write down things that challenged you during the day, the reasons why they were challenging, and anything you tried to do to overcome them. Overcoming challenges builds character and gives you confidence to help you reach your goals.

What Would You Do Differently?

To change your behaviors, you need to be honest with yourself about the things you do not do well. Sometimes you might try to hide from the mistakes you made, because it hurts to face them directly. But you need to face your mistakes in order to learn from your own mistakes.

Ask yourself, "What would I do if I can do some over again today?" You may regret some things that you did that day, but the sense of regret can give you the power to avoid making the same mistakes again.

Inspiring Words, Phrases, Events

Inspiring Words, Phrases, Events

In this section, write down words, phrases or events that inspired you throughout the day. Try to be very positive and look for those things that have helped you during the day, especially in relation to your goal.

If you are conscious of what you really want, you will see things in a different way as before. You will be able to see something that had a good effect on you, even small things happening in your daily life. By recording these things, you realize there are so many good things around you that have great value in helping you achieve your goal.

Case Study - Sumitomo Life Insurance Company

On New Year's Day in 2005, Mr. Koshiro Sato, the executive trainer in the Consulting Department of Sumitomo Life Insurance Company, was trudging along the street near his house, thinking about his past. "I needed a good excuse to help me get through the drudgery of the day," he recalled.

In those days, Mr. Sato was in charge of Sumitomo's on-the-job training course for corporate business. The purpose of the training course was to teach workers without sales experience to be salespeople. The first group of trainees consisted of 16 people, all in their thirties and forties, who belonged to the General Affairs Department, Finance Department or IT Systems Department. Four trainers, including Mr. Sato, were in charge of training the group.

The course would last for six months. In the first three months, the goal was to give the trainees a strong background in sales by letting them experience actual sales, activities and working with a number of companies in Tokyo. During the second three months, they would study to get a license in Financial Planning.

"The first three months were a disaster," Mr. Sato recalled. "The trainees visited many companies in Tokyo without setting up an appointment in advance," he said, "and it just did not work at all. They had neither sales experience nor a prepared list with names of people they planned to visit. They were lost."

Not knowing who to see when they visited a company, the trainees had few opportunities to give a successful sales talk. They had a tough time. "The trainees felt easily beaten and soon lost their confidence," said Mr. Sato.

Somehow, the inaugural members survived the training and became salespeople. The second group of trainees, however, had a much harder time than the inaugural members. After three months had passed, the second group made only one-quarter of the sales that the inaugural members did.

"What are we doing wrong?" they asked, "Why are we getting such miserable results?" Mr. Sato wondered the same thing. He became irritated and was often very stern with the other trainers. The relationship between the other trainers got worse, and Mr. Sato had no idea what to do. He felt as if he was lost in a maze and could not find a way out.

Mr. Sato did not feel good at all. He stayed at home during the New Year vacation with his family. When he went out for a walk, he watched the surface of the river that was covered with snow and a thought came to his mind;" I would probably be better off if I just died." He tried to shut off the negative thoughts but they just came back. At-53-years old, he had a lot of experience as a successful salesperson and as an assistant branch chief, but he had completely lost his confidence and his pride was deeply wounded.

One day, one of his senior managers told Mr.

Sato that he heard that Takashi Harada had a great method to help people achieve their goals. Mr. Sato told one of his trainees and she went and bought one of Mr. Harada's books. The book, Harada's bestseller, was "The Winning Ways" (Josho-Kyoiku).

Mr. Sato read the book in one day. "I was very impressed," he said. "In the book, Mr. Harada tells how to set goals in a most understandable way. He has a goal-setting form that is very concrete. I especially agreed with his idea of getting rid of those mental restrictions that prevent us from achieving our goals."

There were two weeks left for the second group of trainees to visit companies when Mr. Sato decided to teach his employees the Harada Method. Knowing time was short, he told the group, "we must do what we can do."

He explained how to write Mr. Harada's goal-setting form and its core concepts to the trainees, and asked them to try the method. "I let the trainees set their own goals, not the goals given by company, but the goals they thought valuable for them and set by their own ideas and will."

The results were outstanding. In two weeks, the trainees got three-quarters of the contracts that new trainees normally get in a year. Mr. Sato was astonished. "That was way beyond my expectations. I just couldn't believe it," he said.

Mr. Sato contacted Mr. Harada and asked to take part in the Harada training school for teachers in Tokyo. "I sincerely admired Mr. Harada for his ideas on setting goals and writing the Long-Term Goal Form, but I especially liked the Open Window 64 Chart. When I tried it, I saw clearly all the problems I had in my hands at that time. I admitted to myself that I was a controversial person, but when I got through working on my Open Window 64 Chart, I found solutions to problems that I never thought about before. I wrote the solutions down on the goal-setting form and realized that now I had found a way to get through them."

Mr. Sato once thought that the problem was the trainees, but then realized the problem was within him. He realized that the fault was all his. "My mindset changed," he admitted.

Before his change in attitude, Mr. Sato was focused almost solely on how much the trainees were selling. It was not working.

"When we focus on the sales numbers, we work for our managers," he said. "We don't work for ourselves. When we don't attain our sales targets, we start to think of many reasons to tell our managers that we tried hard but couldn't live up to what was expected from us. Now I know that we were just telling lies to ourselves."

Mr. Sato felt bad for his earlier trainees, because he realized he did not teach them how to set and achieve their goals. He explained, "it is like when you play golf and lift your head when you try to hit the ball. You care too much on where the golf ball will go instead of keeping your attention on the correct process. Keep your head down, swing correctly, and the ball will go where it should. I wanted sales results. **I told my**

team what to do but did not empower them to learn the right process and set their own plans to be successful. More than anything I just didn't trust my trainees."

The third group of trainees was introduced to the Harada Method at the beginning of their training and closed two times the number of contracts then the first two groups. The fourth group was far better and they got many more contracts. The fifth group produced three times as many results as the first. As the trainees started to do better, Mr. Sato recovered his confidence.

Mr. Sato's team continued to improve their sales training and the trainees continued to do very well. They focused on building up their trainees' spirits. Said Mr. Sato, "sales techniques by themselves are not enough to make a successful salesperson. **When you allow people to set and achieve their own goals, as taught by the Harada Method, people develop new fundamental skills."**

As he taught more trainees the Harada Method, Mr. Sato also discovered the importance of mentors. "We salespeople sometimes lose sight of our goals, and are not sure why we are working so hard. We need someone who cares for us." He tells the other trainers to find things to support the trainees as much as possible.

"I tell the trainers to give trainees positive signs that they care for the trainees," he said. "Also, I tell trainees to find mentors to help them. Anyone can be your mentor - your boss, your trainers, or your customers. I tell trainees to visit their mentors as much as possible, and encourage them to disclose their goals to their mentors as much as possible. Having mentors near you will help you realize your small but important steps to reach to your ultimate goals. Your mentor can be the key to your ultimate success."

Mr. Sato is now much more conscious of how to be a leader. **"Leaders must give their employees and trainees the power to be successful on their own.** Mr. Harada is a leader. He says something vibrant and strong and does it in a timely manner, and he encourages people constantly. That's what we call charisma and every leader needs it."

Mr. Sato once regarded himself as a rather introverted person, and thought there was no way he could be like Mr. Harada, but now he realizes that it is not true. "If you talk to Mr. Harada, you will find him a very sensitive and shy person," says Sato. "But he can play his role as a powerful and strong trainer when he teaches people how to set goals. He makes a great effort to encourage us. In truth, we can all be like Mr. Harada. Mr. Harada attests to us that the power to succeed is attainable by making continuous effort."

Mr. Sato often works on his Open Window 64 Chart and updates his goal-setting sheet. He feels he has no need to take "evasion tactics" anymore. He used to wonder if he should go back to work as a branch manager and not be a trainer, but now he is happy to work as a trainer helping trainees achieve their goals.

He bashfully but confidently said, "I used to think I did my best, but somewhere in my heart I worked with a degree of resignation. I felt irritated because things just did not work as I intended, but now I have changed. I like myself as I am." He remembered the day when he stared at the surface of the snowy river with no hope for the future. Things have changed greatly since then. Now he is sure of himself and in his ability to help others.

Chapter 19 - Work with a Coach/Mentor

> "The difference between the possible and the impossible lies in a person's determination." - Tommy Lasorda, former Los Angeles Dodgers manager

In Chapter 15 we determined the kind of support you need to attain our goals. Here we will look more at the importance of working with a coach or mentor. This is an important principle of the method. Although you like to think you can do everything by yourself, having a great coach makes a tremendous difference in how quickly you realize your goals. Coaches can foresee obstacles in our path and give us suggestions to overcome them. They inspire us, and encourage us when we need help. They are able to observe us from the outside and tell us what we need to do to improve.

In the early 1960's, I owned a data processing company in New York City. At that time playing golf was popular and I thought it was important that I learn how to play. Every Thursday morning I would go out and play, but I was terrible. I could hit beautiful hooks and shanks but rarely could I hit the ball straight. I thought if I just practiced really hard, I would learn how to play well. I was wrong. I played and played, but never broke 100, and even started to hate the sport. The last day I golfed, I played eight holes and lost nine balls.

Years later, I met John Schlee, a former professional golfer, who won the Hawaiian Open and came in second in the US Open. John wanted to work with Jim Swartz[31] and me. He wanted us to teach top executives the power of Lean. The plan was that Jim and I would teach Lean in the morning, and he would give golf lessons to the attendees in the afternoon. It sounded like a great idea. Before we ran the event together, though, he wanted to teach me how to play golf.

John took me out to the driving range, showed me how to place my hands on the shaft, told me to keep my head down and showed me how to swing. He only coached me for a few minutes, and I started to hit balls straight down the narrow fairway in front of me. It was a miracle! I never did that before. I realized what a fool I had been for not taking lessons earlier.

Why hadn't I found a coach before? When I owned the data processing company, my ego was huge and it prevented me from taking lessons from a coach - I thought I could learn it on my own. My ego took away all of the fun I could have had golfing.

One of the principles of the Harada Method is to work with a coach who can review your work and see that you stay on course. A coach will help you fill out the forms, and give you honest feedback on what you write. A coach will ask you questions pertaining to your goals to help you overcome your own resistance to change.

---

[31] Jim Swartz is the author of "Seeing David in the Stone," "The Hunters and the Hunted" and is an amazing management consultant.

It is not easy for me to work with a coach. It requires me to let someone else see what I might not be doing correctly in my life – this can be humbling. But I have noticed that when I do accept the idea that a coach will see my daily diaries, it has caused me to complete them correctly – I put a lot more effort into filling them out completely. Without a coach, I can easily avoid doing it properly, saying to myself that I am tired and will do it later. With a coach, I pressure myself to complete the forms precisely the way Mr. Harada would want me to do it.

When you start using the method, you should talk to your coach for a few minutes each day to go over the forms and talk about any questions you might have. As soon as you get into the habit of writing your Harada forms and doing what you need to do to succeed, meeting with your coach once a week is sufficient.

Time Doesn't Flow from the Past to the Future

In the Harada system you look into the future. You define what you want to be and visualize that it has already happened. You need to have a very strong picture of our future success. You put yourself into the future and look back to the current moment and see a gap. You now feel responsible to do something to fill the gap. And since in our mind you have already succeeded, you then have to just write down the steps you took to get there.

Some of Mr. Harada's students and clients have difficulty in creating their vision of what they want in their future. The coach then helps to draw out what they want to create for their future.

The coach's job is to also be responsible for helping their mentees avoid failure. The coach takes ownership as much as the mentee does. They work together, to accomplish the goal.

One technique from Mr. Harada that might be helpful is to write down 10 possible goals that you would like to accomplish. Then show your list to your friends, family, boss and coach and get their input. Then pick the best goal for you to pursue. I did a variation of this when I sold Productivity Inc./Press over ten years ago when I wanted to start something new. I wrote down actually 11 things that came to me to start a new business. I then asked my closest advisors to look at my list. I listened. I liked their advice and from their suggestions I started to become a writer with my first book "The Idea Generator," which launched me into a new career.

I taught a class recently to a group of employees at a very large organization. I worked very hard to teach them the Harada Method but it was very hard for me as a few of them would just not believe in their own ability to set new goals and to accomplish them. They had previous trainings in their organization but frustratingly they never were able to put those new concepts to real use. Management would send them to the training class with the thought of helping them improve at their jobs, but management did not know how to act as coaches to inspire and lead their employees to internalize and experience the new knowledge.

Harada's challenge while he was still working at the school was how to coach one-to-one with over 600 students. He couldn't afford to hire more coaches to work with him. The Long-Term Form and Daily Dairy became his instruments to be able to coach many students and to help them to close the gap between them and their goal. The forms are the student's personal coach. The student then begins to wear the hat of a coach for them self. Mr. Harada was able to quickly review each student's forms and give feedback and comments. Initially, the students' forms were not that good but Mr. Harada would write his comments in red ink and he would go back and forth with the students. The forms helped communicate to the students how they were doing and fostered greater passion to do a better job.

As Harada explained, "By looking at my student's Long-Term Form, I could understand them very well and how they envisioned their future, getting there and the excitement generated in them. 'I think it is possible,' they would say. I could see if they really meant it. It also showed what help they needed mentally, skill-building, physical conditioning and in their life.

Tips for coaching

"The difference between a successful person and others is not a lack of strength, not a lack of knowledge, but rather a lack of will." - Vince Lombardi, former football coach, Green Bay Packers

What a Coach Does:

1. A coach is a mentor who supports, inspires, guides, leads, encourages, and brings out the best from his or her client. A coach is a change agent.
2. The coach meets with the client daily (if possible) to observe that the person is staying on target to reach their goals. Coaches know what "true north"[32] is, and they help their clients stay focused.
3. Coaches ask questions that relate to attaining the clients' goals. They help clients remove obstacles and overcome their resistance to change.
4. Coaches create awareness by observing clients' habits, routines and improvement efforts.
5. Coaches lead their clients toward a goal.

Things to Remember When You are a Coach

1. Seat angles - Avoid sitting face-to-face, but try sitting side by side or 90 degrees
2. Distance - Keep the distance between the client at least 60 centimeters)
3. Give sympathetic signals - Nod, smile and look at the client's eyes.
4. Pygmalion Effect - Believe that the clients will succeed and help them make it happen.
5. Pacing - Match the speed of the client's speech, the tone of the voice, rhythm and breath. For

---

[32] True North is attaining the ideal state.

example, if the client speaks slowly, the coach would speak slowly as well.

6. Mirroring - Subtly imitate the client's posture.
7. Backtracking - Repeat the points the client has mentioned. For example, when the client says, "the goal is $300,000 in sales" the coach says, "Wow, the goal is $300,000 in sales. That's amazing!"

Chapter 20 - Revise the Monthly Long-Term Goal Setting Form

"I rewrote the ending of Farewell to Arms, the last page of it, 39 times before I was satisfied." - Ernest Hemingway

Once a month, it is good to go back and look at your Long-Term Goal Form and 64-Chart to check off the things you accomplished and add and revise tasks that you would like to achieve in the future.

You should have both a long-term goal - something that will make you feel successful for virtually the rest of your life - as well as a short-term goal, things you would like to accomplish for the next month or two. You should go through the entire Harada process for both your short-term and long-term goals.

Harada says, "everyone can be successful." This is absolutely true, but you have to want it and you have to be willing to work for it. No one can tell you what is success; you decide that for yourself. But, keep in mind that if you work for an organization that is paying your salary, you should try to pick a goal that is good for you and good for your organization at the same time.

Chapter 21 - Teams, Self-Reliance and Developing People

> "Talent wins games, but teamwork and intelligence wins championships."
> - Michael Jordan

Japanese companies are noted for being team-oriented, but the Harada Method focuses on the self-reliance of each individual in an organization. How can you reconcile these two viewpoints?

While the Harada Method does focus on the performance of the individual and making a person self-reliant, this does not clash with what we think of in the West as the Japanese model. An organization or a team is comprised of individuals; so when each employee's performance improves so does the entire organization. Japanese companies already know this very well. They are team-oriented, but they focus a great deal on each individual's development, productivity and happiness.

A year ago, I visited a Hino Motors plant, outside of Tokyo, that manufactured trucks and buses. While walking along the assembly line, I noticed a supervisor videoing a worker. This is often done in Japan, since developing people to be efficient is the primary job for a supervisor. The supervisor will take a video of the same employee working on several vehicles and will study the video, looking for variations and ways to improve performance. The supervisor will then get together with the worker to determine how to improve his or her performance. By very closely studying each individual's performance, Japanese companies have greatly improved their overall company's performance.

Using the Harada Method to encourage people to reach their highest potential, therefore, does not in any way contradict the idea of team building. Once again, a sports analogy is appropriate. On a basketball team, for example, you have different positions and roles for the various players. Some of the players will always be the superstars and be very difficult to replace. Others are players who work hard but are not as visible as the stars. They might be easier to replace than a superstar, but you still want to develop them to their fullest potential because it makes the whole team stronger. The same is true for a company.

Many companies are reluctant to spend money on training. If you have 10,000 employees and it costs $300 per person for a training course, that is $3,000,000, and you can never be quite sure what the benefit will be from the training. But, if you can get people excited about picking something at work to improve their skills, you can find the right training for them and they will work on their own to be successful, like winning their own personal Olympics. As Jeremy Green, an associate of mine, said:

**"Training is Expensive, but Developing People is Free."
Jeremy Greene, Phd.**

Today, many Japanese companies are using the Harada Method as a key process to get their employees excited about lifelong learning and continuous improvement. The Harada Method provides a disciplined, rigorous process for learning and achieving success for every position at every level.

> **"I love the people from US Synthetic. We just honored their company at our award ceremony a couple of weeks ago in Jacksonville, Florida. They are one of the best examples of a company that is really genuinely committed to its people."** - Robert Miller, Executive Director
> **The Shingo Prize**

What does it mean, "genuinely committed to its people?" Every company is made up of a diverse group of people gathered together to produce products and deliver services. The higher the quality of these goods and services the greater the chance for success. Survival in this highly competitive world depends on how well people can work together and how well they bring out the best from each other. We no longer live in the jungle or the dark ages and in this country the age of slavery is over and yet strangely there are still companies that do not treat their employees with the highest level of respect.

Very often, when I talk about the success of Japanese management someone will say that the Japanese are naturally team oriented while we in America are individualistic. I don't fully agree with this. I do think the idea is misused as if we in America are not capable of working well in teams. With good leadership we can be very effective team players. The Harada Method can be equally effective with individuals as it can with teams setting and obtaining common goals.

Case Study - Chugai Pharmaceuticals

A year ago, I led a study mission to Japan with about 28 people from the Shingo Prize group at Utah State University. We spent one day with Mr. Harada, during which he lectured to the group and also took us to one of his clients, Chugai Pharmaceuticals. At Chugai, the manager of human resources spoke to us about the company's corporate goals and how Mr. Harada helped them set up a mentor/mentee program.

To be competitive, the manager said, Chugai needed to manufacture medicines at the lowest cost possible. However, cutting costs alone was not enough to survive.

Previously, Chugai managers had focused mainly on developing products, placing less emphasis on how quickly they developed them. Advances in technology and competition meant that the company needed to develop new products faster. This required a new way of thinking. "The new issues for us were how to match the development of new products with the manufacturing process as well as how to develop people quickly in order to meet the new demands," said the manager

Employees needed to be trained differently. "We needed a system to support the employees," the manager explained. "In the past, we were developing people for a stable production environment, but with our global market initiative, we needed competent people who could lead new products. Just taking orders correctly was no longer good enough. We needed people who could think, take actions independently and, in the terminology of the Harada Method, be self-reliant workers."

Traditionally, Japanese HR managers focused solely on developing employees' expertise in a particular area, but Chugai also wanted to develop its employees' interpersonal skills such as leadership.

"In the past, the employees might have had a broader perspective," he said, "but now we needed people to be narrowly focused and also to be able to work together. Since everyone's job had become so specialized, our success depended on cooperation and teamwork."

After looking around for the right system to develop these traits in people, Chugai chose the Harada Method. "With the Harada Method, we now have the ability to prepare and reflect when we work on a project. More importantly, we focus on developing people. Fifty percent of a managers' evaluations are based on how well they develop people."

Chugai uses the Harada Method as the basis for its mentoring system for new employees. When new employees are hired, typically in May, they work out with the company a set of very challenging growth goals to accomplish by the end of the year. Because the goals are so difficult to achieve, the employees must focus their efforts every day to reach them.

Each person is assigned a mentor to help guide him or her. The mentoring system normally lasts for one year. During that time, mentors communicate with their

Time	Plans	Results		Key Goal	Name: Ms. Kotoe Kanda
					Today's Date: 3/13/2012 — Today's Phrase: Schedule for the day — Things to do today

 # 82 Mentor – Mentee Diary Example:

Time	Plans	Results
5		
6		
7	Wake up	6:30 Woke up
8	8:30-Clean	Washed & cleaned
9		Went to bank
10	Go Shopping	
11	Went to work	11:30 Left to work
N	12:30 start work	Started to work
1		Ran 1st machine
2		
3	Break	3:30 Break
4		Ran 1st machine
5		
6		
7		
8		Wrote journal
9	9:15 go home	
10		
11		

Tasks for Today
1) Have a lunch with other coworkers
2) Learn Quickly how to deal with a problem
3) Caution with mistakes in writing
4) Remember to sanitize my hands
5) Answer aloud

Good Things Noticed Today
1) I'm getting used to type in labels.
2) Do you get the total number if the number in lot is the same with PR and BS?

What Would You Do Differently?
I did not check enough the container display. I only checked the container number and lot number but did not look carefully enough at the pallet number. I'm sorry.

Positively Inspiring Words, Phrases, Events
It was a good experience for me to work in a small team. I would like to handle my work more quickly.

Questions to Mentor
Should I be in the labeler team before pulling things out regularly?

Copyrighted 2011 by Harada Institute of Education & PCS Inc. All Rights Reserved

mentees almost daily. They discuss work progress and any other issue that might come up. One of the tools they use to improve their communication is the Harada Daily Diary.

Part of the daily diary kept by the new employees are extra sheets to record observations, instructions, reminders, problems and other things to help them on the job and also those things they want to discuss with their mentors. This is one example:

Mentor - Mentee Diary - Mentor writes some advice with a red pen - affirmation

1: Date 3/13/2012
2: Colleting PRs
    In transition, I collect PRs from the ball into the bag.
    I collect PR as loss from the supply line. ->I will leave the memo in the transition checklist.

3: I thought Mr. Murase in PR team was not surprised with plunger stopper once I get used to BD.
4: When I finish the lot:
*With the three more butch left, I will report to the next procedure team and make sure everything was pulled out from the system.
I will write the procedure finish time + Check the broken glasses
I will write down the number of manufactured products and defects
I will calculate the total number of troubles
I will close the empty columns with an oblique line.
I will remember to reset the machine.
I will be careful not to mix up with pallet number
5: The overall procedure was slow, and I delayed preparing the display and the lot transition check. I want to be quick in each action so that I won't cause troubles to others.
6: When the pallet number changed, you have to change the row.

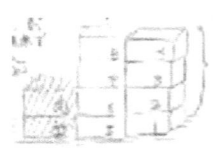

7: After piling up four boxes, you have to change the row. The maximum number on the each row is four.
8:        *I am sorry to mix up with the pallet numbers. Once different tasks than usual come into play, I froze and make mistakes. I want to prepare and review by using this note.
         *I want to be careful in labeling, without forgetting writing in or putting the old labels.
         * The first machine had a weird sound during the regular procedure. Was that because of its bearing? That' right!
         * I could not meet with Mr. Suzuki from 3T. I wanted to give him a thank-you card. What should I do?
         * Troubleshooting
<Separating BS> Where do I look?

"The more trust you get, more responsibility you own. Now no one blames your mistake. So learn now from them as much as possible."

The Harada Diary teaches mentees the importance of daily preparation and reflection. Before starting work, the mentees organize their time and prioritize the tasks they need to get done that day. After work, mentees spend time writing down how the day went and what they learned. Chugai added a sheet to the diary to give employees space to write extra reflections.

Mentors look over the diaries and give feedback to the mentees by writing comments in the diary and through face-to-face meetings. Overall, employees like using the Diary. Although it is not required, most people continue to use the diary even after the first year.

Chugai found that the company attracted better people because of its reputation for developing employees. During our visit to the company, both a mentor and a mentee shared their Harada Method experience with us.

The mentor who spoke had a master's degree in pharmacology and was a certified pharmacist. He had been at the company for four years and worked on the production line as an operator. "I came to Chugai because I wanted to contribute to the health in our society," he said. "I want to be an expert in developing the manufacturing process." He knew he could gain that expertise by working at the company.

The mentee also had a sense of purpose. She had studied chemistry and wanted to use her knowledge in a technical field that makes new medicines and beautiful products. She also wanted to work with a company with a solid background. The HR person at Chugai who interviewed her impressed her so much she decided to join the company. "My goal is to deepen my understanding of what I am doing, to be an expert with my machine and to do something different in the future."

Both of the employees that spoke had clear goals for their futures. They were dedicated to learning and improving skills that would strengthen the company.

By using the Harada Method, Chugai is developing employees who are able to think, to solve problems and to be better leaders. With better-trained employees, the company is able to produce more products more quickly (and at lower costs). The company has gained a reputation for growing its employees and now attracts more talented people. Chugai has a bright future ahead of it.

Chapter 22 - The People Side of Lean - Looking into the Future and Creating an Ideal Workplace

> "Choose a job you love, and you will never have to work a day in your life."
> - Confucius

The Harada Method compliments the work of Dr. Shigeo Shingo and Taiichi Ohno by addressing the "People Side of Lean." Virtually every company today is attempting to be Lean, but very few know how to achieve it. The Harada Method can be used to gain full cooperation for a company's Lean efforts. When people know how to take full responsibility for their own lives and be self-reliant, with the support of management, they can become like an arrow - clearly focused on how to be successful personally and professionally.

I taught recently in Salt Lake City to 200 managers, engineers and sales people at Dover Corporation, with a number of their group presidents in the audience. The company has 35,000 employees worldwide. It was probably my best talk ever, and they invited me back to teach around 25 of their managers the Harada Method and to certify four of their trainers to teach other employees. One of Dover's companies is US Synthetic, probably one of the best Lean companies in America. They get 60 improvement ideas per worker per year simply by empowering their employees to offer small suggestions to make their work easier and more interesting. Last year US Synthetic won the Shingo

Prize. Here is already a great company wanting to be better and they recognize that the Harada Method is the missing element in their development of people. I often find this to be true, that a very good company wants to get better but the companies that really need to get better find excuses not to change.

There is an old saying, "A chain is only as strong as its weakest link." Every worker is an important "link" in your company and must be part of the continuous improvement process. We can see the importance of strengthening each member on a baseball, basketball or football team, but somehow forget this in our companies. To be successful in this fiercely competitive world, you must harness the talents of every single worker.

In November 2011, I spoke at a conference in Singapore. I came back to America just fascinated with the country's success story. Singapore is one of the most self-reliant countries in the world. In 1959, Singapore had a GDP[33] of $400 per person. According to the International Monetary Fund, in 2011, the figure had risen to $59,936. For comparison purposes, America's is only $48,147.

Singapore has no natural resources except people and a great deep harbor. What Singapore's leaders did over the last 50 years was to focus on bringing in high value-added jobs. They focused on education and being

---

[33] **Gross domestic product (GDP)** is the market value of all officially recognized final goods and services produced within a country in a given period. GDP per capita is often considered an indicator of a country's standard of living.

the best in whatever they did. They didn't want the "cheap labor" jobs like China and other Asian countries - a decision that paid large dividends to Singapore's economic development.

> "The new industrial society is giving way to the one based on knowledge. The new divide in the world will be between those with the knowledge and those without. We must learn to be part of the knowledge-based world, with the best man and woman for the job. To survive, we had to be better organized and more efficient and competitive than the rest." -
> Lee Kuan Yew, former Singapore Prime Minister

Skill Charts

I visited a Yokogawa Electric plant, while I was in Singapore that produced control systems for Airbus jets. The plant was a great example of a company utilizing all of the tools and techniques of the Toyota Production System. There were no conveyor belts or assembly lines in the plant. Everyone I saw was doing highly-skilled tasks in their work cells, building the complete components, and not just doing simple repetitive tasks. On one wall, I saw a skill chart.

A skill chart at Yokogawa Electric Corporation, Singapore

Japanese companies have used skill charts for years. Traveling around Japan, I would often see skill charts on factory walls listing all the skills needed in the plant, and each employee's name and the skills they had mastered. Many of these skills are certified, and often the training is conducted by one of the company's highly skilled workers. Management using the skill charts inspired the workers to continually improve themselves.

Consider creating a skill's development program in your company. Define all of the needed skills and set-up certification programs to get employees to become the best at what they do. Your teachers can be the person with the highest skills in each area. You might be surprised at how much your employees learn just by being given the opportunity.

Chapter 23 - Become a Master

"The **kaizen system** of incremental improvement owes much to traditional Japanese **craftsmen**. No one sits down and teaches an apprentice all the techniques he needs to become a master. He starts out as a minarai, a watching apprentice, and **learns by watching**. First, he is given menial jobs around the workshop. After a time, he may get the chance to do a trivial part of the process. Later he may purchase his own tools and try things out in his spare time. He gradually gains more responsibility. At no time does the master specifically "teach" him anything. It is up to the apprentice to **"steal the art,"** to figure out for himself/herself what the master is doing to get the right results. Over time, the apprentice develops a technique like the master's, but also all his own. Each person sees the process with a fresh eye, **observing the master but learning for himself** how to make the process work." - Japan Intercultural Consulting

In the 1800s, many people were artisans. Young people had to go through an apprenticeship for many years with a master craftsperson, and they ended up with a very valuable skill. Between 1880 and 1900, Frederick Taylor developed the concept of the "division of labor" and the "simplification of work." Henry Ford used the concept of de-skilling, putting people onto an assembly line, having them repeat very simple tasks over and over again.

If you worked for Ford in those days, your job might be to tighten eight screws on an automobile, the same eight screws on each automobile, for eight to ten hours a day, every day. The work was so boring that Ford had to hire 963 people to get 100 to stay on the job and had to double their wage. Ford's system was effective, and his company became the richest in America. Many companies emulated his model, which was great for shareholders but not so good for workers.

You would think work has improved since then, but this is not always the case. On my last visit to a Lexus plant in Tahara, Japan, I watched SUV's being assembled. I noticed a person on the assembly line reaching overhead to tighten bolts on every automobile. I walked over to watch the worker and spoke to a supervisor nearby. "How long will he do that job," I asked? The supervisor said, "He does that on every car, around 500 today. He will do that same job probably for the next three months, maybe even for the next six months."

Observing this worker at Lexus doing this repetitive work confused me. Toyota is noted for their two pillars for success: Just-in-Time (Lean) and "Respect for People." What kind of respect is given to a worker when he does the same simple repetitive task over and over again?

Two days after visiting Lexus, I visited a Canon factory in Toride, Japan where they assemble imaging products and copiers. Ten years ago when I visited this plant, there had been a conveyor belt with around 40 workers standing on the line assembling copiers. The workers did very simple, repetitive tasks, over and over again. During this current visit, however, I watched one worker in a cell assemble an entire digital copier. The manager told me the worker would install 540 parts in 178 minutes on her own, with a 30% higher productivity rate than the conveyor belt. When the woman finished assembling the copier, she said, "I feel as if I just made a new baby." What pride people can have in their work when their responsibilities and skills are continuously improved!

Ironically, it was ex-Toyota managers that taught Canon how to set up these new cells. Canon has now converted all of their 54 manufacturing plants from conveyor belts and assembly lines to cellular manufacturing. The people that can make the entire copier by themselves are called "supermeisters[34]." Not every worker can assemble an entire copier. It does take time - sometimes years - for people to develop this level of mastery, but everyone is given the opportunity to grow.

As I traveled more in Japan, I found many other companies recognizing the need to develop their people into artisans, to be self-reliant in order to compete with the low-cost Asian companies in China, Thailand, India, etc. Toyota itself is also moving in the direction of creating master technicians. At the Tahara Lexus plant, where I had seen the worker tightening the eight bolts,

---

[34] **Supermeister** is one who has mastered all the processes. Meister is a German word meaning master.

the company recently started a mastery program to certify, promote and recognize people with very high skills.

Artisans to Artisans - Coming Full Circle

Over the last ten years, a lot of the repetitive work in factories has gone to Mexico, China and other Asian countries, while many workers in America who lack developed skills, are unable to find gainful employment. With the assembly line based on simplified work, it was easy to take that human work and automate it, have robots and other machines replace people in the workplace, or send the work to China.

To compete against the "low cost" labor countries, the industrialized nations are beginning to realize that their economic survival rests on people once again becoming artisans or highly skilled workers. Thus, it seems we are going full circle from the artisans in the 19th century to repetitive tasks to automation and back to artisans in this 21st century.

In fact, I believe that Germany today is highly successful in the global market because they still have a very strong apprentice program developing master craftspeople.

When I was ready to enter high school, we had a choice to go to a school preparing us for college or to learn a skilled trade. Many students went on to choose a trade. Today there are much fewer trade schools. We do have a shortage of skilled craftspeople in America. Hopefully, people will recognize early on how the Harada

Method can help young people pick skilled trades for their future profession.

Imagine your company in the future. Imagine that you removed your conveyor belts and assembly lines like Canon did and converted them to manufacturing cells. Within each cell, instead of the worker doing boring and repetitive work, they are now multi-skilled building entire modules.

Imagine that there is a better way for your workers to do more creative work, be more fulfilled, be more secure and also have your corporation achieve its goals?

Repetitive Work Does Not Have to Be Bad

On another study mission to Japan, I visited Kokusan Denki, a Hitachi group plant, and watched a middle-aged man in the factory doing very simple, repetitive work. To me it was deadly. He put a small metal part into a machine and hit a button. The machine then worked on the part. Then the man took the part out and replaced it with another one. While I watched him, suddenly, he slammed his hands against the machine, shouted loudly and looked as if he was absolutely crazy. He looked just the way I would have felt if I had to do that job over and over again, every day of the week. After screaming, calmly he went back to work doing the same repetitive task.

A few minutes later, I walked down the line and watched a middle-aged woman holding a small motor in one hand, very carefully soldering wires to the motor. It took her a few minutes to solder each motor. She then picked up another motor and did the same thing again. She looked totally different from the previous man. Her job required great focus and concentration and she was very skilled at what she was doing.

Like the first worker, the woman also was doing repetitive work. Unlike the first worker, she looked totally at peace with her work. It was obvious to me the difference between the two jobs. I even asked the woman, "how do you like your job?" She answered that she was very happy with what she was doing. I knew it was true. The man's job was totally boring, but the women's job required great concentration and dexterity.

This was a great lesson for me, to see both people in the factory doing repetitive work. The woman's job required a high degree of skill and thus had meaning and gave dignity to her, while the man's job was not designed for a human being. Management should see the difference when designing what work needs to be done.

As part of a leadership development session during the trip, participants were asked to reflect on their work lives and share what they would have done differently. A retired CEO replied, "I had a major opportunity to help make my employees' lives better. I could have invested in building my people's skills. I used to think, 'why should I invest in people when they will one day get up and leave the company?' I messed up. Their success would have been our success. I am truly sorry now."

Monozukuri and Hitozukuri

One of the main focal points in Japan today is for workers to become masters in some discipline. Since Japan cannot compete against the low labor rate in

China, India and elsewhere in Asia, Japanese companies must produce high value-added products with highly skilled workers. In a number of companies, you hear the words monozukuri (build great products), hitozukuri (build great people to build those great products), self-determined, autonomous and self-reliant. The Harada Method works perfectly with this concept. Uniquely different using the Harada Method, instead of just telling people what to do, you can share your organizational goals you want to achieve and ask them how they would accomplish it.

Monozukuri and hitozukuri are not just confined to manufacturing. They are applicable in other fields too. I love sushi, and when I go to Japan I often eat at a sushi restaurant near where my wife and I have a house in Kirishima City, Kyushu. On one visit in November 2011, I ate a wonderful piece of Maguro from the belly of the world's finest and most expensive tuna also known as Toro. It is one of the more expensive items on the menu, prized for its taste, texture, and scarcity. We have been going to this restaurant for years, but this was the first time the chef looked at me as a prized customer and made sure that I got only the best fish he had to offer.

While we were talking, the chef told me that it takes from nine to twelve years to learn how to be a really good sushi chef, with the knowledge to buy the right fish and prepare it the right way. A good example of if you take the time to build great people (hitozukuri), you will be able to build great products (monozukuri).

In Japan you can spend over $20 for just one piece of Toro.

Mr. Nakamura, the man who introduced me to Mr. Harada's work, told me about a small Japanese company that made a metal funnel for the last Japanese satellite sent out to space to study the dust surrounding an asteroid. To lathe the metal funnel required such precision and sensitivity that only a person who spent a multitude of years honing his skills could attain. This is the type of work that cannot be outsourced to a low-cost country using unskilled labor.

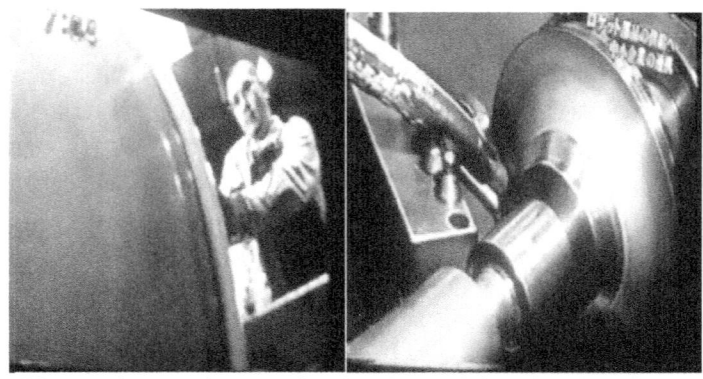

The artisan who made the funnel for the satellite was both skilled and self-reliant.

At virtually every company I have visited in Japan recently, the managers talk about how important it is to have highly-skilled, self-reliant people who can build great products. One example is Kyowa, a company that makes universal joints for Toyota. Kyowa developed a completely new process to make its products, changing over from hot forging to cold forging. At first, Toyota's managers did not want to buy the products from them. However, three months later they came back and said they had no choice, because Kyowa was able to manufacture their product with tolerances no other company could come close to. You can imagine the leverage Kyowa had in its negotiations with Toyota over the prices for their universal joints! Kyowa was successful because it had highly-skilled workers who knew how to build better products.

Every Employee is Capable of Innovation

I heard the president of Kokuyo, a major stationery manufacturer in Japan that employs 5,000 people, tell his employees, "When you go home from work, stop at a stationery store and watch the interaction between the clerk and the customer. Look for ideas on new products and how we can improve our existing products for the customers' needs."

One young female employee stopped at a stationary store on the way home from work and observed a clerk talking with a customer about paper glue. The clerk told the customer, "We have two kinds of paper glue a glue stick or liquid glue." The clerk brought up two problems, "The glue stick dries out and the liquid glue is messy and difficult to apply accurately."[35]

The employee came back to the office the very next day, gathered her colleagues together, and reported what she had observed. The group then brainstormed the problem with the glue and came up with a new product, which looks like a tape dispenser, except that the "tape" is covered with very tiny bubbles of liquid glue. When you press the tape against the paper and draw it towards you, the bubbles break and the glue is applied in a straight line without any mess. Kokuyo came up with this million-dollar product just by encouraging all of its workers to help. You never know where the next great idea can come from!

Why Training is Important

For the past 30 years, with a few exceptions, my books and workshops have focused on helping managers teach their employees how to reduce costs, how to implement the Lean tools, how to improve the process, and how to eliminate non-value adding wastes. But very little was on how to improve leadership skills of managers to lead the Lean efforts and the competency and success of the individuals that work within

---

[35] How often do people in your company tell customers about potential problems?

organizations. Now that I have learned about the Harada Method, it seems ironic that my earlier life focused so little on making managers more competent, and higher skilled.

Recently in Montreal, I gave a talk to around 24 senior executives from many of the leading companies in Canada. I asked them to tell me the number of hours they invested in training, outside of on-the-job training. I asked them to raise their hand if they gave 24 or more hours per year. Only one hand went up. If we are to compete internationally with China and India, we must change our perspective and invest in building our talent. When I first went to Japan many years ago, the mindset was that every worker should become an engineer. We need a similar mindset here today.

Companies are strong when their employees are strong, but so little is invested in training people. Companies will hire competency from colleges and other organizations, but rarely do they invest deeply in their own people. When you do go to school, you are asked to continuously learn new ideas and develop your skills, but when you leave school and go to work you often stop that process of self-development. It is funny, that most managers want continuous improvement of the process and the product, but they do not encourage continuous improvement from their employees.

Mr. Harada recognizes this problem and makes a dynamic switch by putting the burden on the individuals to seek out their own training. The old Chinese proverb is very appropriate: "Give a man a fish and you feed him for a day. Teach a man to fish and you feed him for a lifetime."

Case Study - A Store Manager at Watami

This is a story from Mr. Moriyuki, a manager at Harada Education Institute in Osaka, Japan.

Before coming to the Harada Education Institute, Mr. Moriyuki worked as a store manager at Watami, a Japanese-style pub on Dotonbori Street, one of the busiest in downtown Osaka City. When the Dotonbori store opened in 2000, it was jam-packed virtually every night. By 2007, when Mr. Moriyuki became the store manager, the boom had passed. There were a lot of competing stores in the area and the sales at the store were slowing. The previous store manager tried many different things to turn the situation around, but sales were not recovering when Mr. Moriyuki took over.

Mr. Moriyuki noticed that the right kind of energy was lacking in his employees. **The first thing he did was to train his employees to be self-reliant, so that they could make the right decisions for the customers and for the store.** He wanted them all to feel jointly responsible for turning around the situation. At a company meeting, he presented his own ideas and philosophy to the employees, and then asked them what they could do to move the store forward.

To improve the employees' attitudes, Mr. Moriyuki tried many things. He began cleaning the locker room with his employees. He asked them to be punctual, and made it a rule of the store to come to work 15 minutes early. This would allow all of the employees to get together before the start of the day to talk about ways they could improve each customer's experience.[36] Also, he carefully asked them to improve their appearances, by taking off their mufflers and sunglasses when they entered the store, for example. To build morale, he asked them to greet each other cheerfully when they came to work.

To build the employees' skills, Mr. Moriyuki went over the manuals with them, and encouraged them to remember each point. He wanted them to understand everything 100%. He constantly reminded them to follow all of the manuals details about how to serve dishes, and how to say hello with a smile to the customers. Nothing was too small.

Mr. Moriyuki also spent a lot of time teaching key employees how to be his stand-in when he was not in the store.

Having taught the employees the principles of self-reliance, Mr. Moriyuki set performance goals for the

---

[36] In Japan, I have seen often employees in stores and in other companies meeting and gathering together for around five to ten minutes before opening their doors to customers or starting production. In the morning, the manager is trying to motivate his associates to really give their upmost efforts to please customers or to make great products. In the evening, the manager is both complimenting employees for their daily efforts and also having them share problems that occurred during the day. Employees will present their problems and talk about possible solutions to prevent the reoccurrence of the problems.

store. He set a goal to attain 19,000,000 yen in sales in December of 2007. When he announced his goal at the meeting with all of the other managers, he noticed cynical and icy eyes looking at him. Everyone knew that the goal he set was a crazy one because the average sales of his store had been only 10,000,000 yen per month.

Ignoring their skepticism, Mr. Moriyuki wrote out his goals and action plans, and completed the Harada Goal Form with all of the managers and many of the employees.[37]

Mr. Moriyuki set one more goal that month. He wanted to break the one-day sales record from the previous seven years. He announced his goals and ideas to his employees. They were very surprised, but said they would totally support his desire to achieve the goal.

The best one-day sales record at the time was 1,100,000 yen. Moriyuki knew the best opportunity to break the record would be December 31, when the Dotonbori Street store would be crowded with people planning to celebrate the New Year - a major gift-giving holiday in Japan.

Everyone prepared for the big event, using the commonly prepared Harada Goal Form to anticipate potential and expected problems. They prepared thoroughly and faced the situation optimistically.

---

[37] The Harada Method can be used by individuals to attain their own goals, and it can also be used by groups to attain organizational goals.

When December 31 arrived, the store was crowded with people until closing time. The last person who came to the store asked Mr. Moriyuki to please give him a glass of beer while he was waiting for his wife to finish shopping. Mr. Moriyuki got the man a glass of beer and some boiled soybeans. The sale pushed the store's sales to 1,105,000 yen - a new record. It brought the total sales for December to 19,800,000 yen, also a record. Moriyuki credited the accomplishments to the team's thorough preparations.

Due to the remarkable success of the store, Mr. Moriyuki was assigned to a much larger store two months later. That kind of transfer was very rare, but Mr. Moriyuki had earned it.

Chapter 24 - Questions from a Certified Student

> If you hire people just because they can do a job, they'll work for your money. But if you hire people who believe what you believe, they'll work for you with blood and sweat and tears." - Simon Sinek

Girish V Datar, President of Alignstream in Pune, India (info@alignstream.com) called and told me he wanted to come from India to attend my Harada Method certification workshop and he wanted to teach the Harada Method in India. I told him not to come. "It is too expensive to come all the way from India and pay in US dollars. (One dollar equals 55.27 rupees and means that Girish's real cost in Indian dollars is a fortune.) It is too much of a gamble for you. You might not be able to learn enough in one week to set up a new business in India." He insisted, took the gamble, came over, was certified, and I am sure he will be an excellent instructor. Since graduating almost every week he sends me a set of questions. He really tests me for I do not have all of the answers for him. But, Mr. Harada has been very kind to fill in when I can't answer the question.

I can teach a workshop, then ask the participants if they have any questions. At times, I feel as if I am pulling teeth to get anyone to respond. I wonder how they can sit with me and not come up with dozens of questions. People are just embarrassed. They mentally go back to their schools days and are afraid to ask stupid questions of their teacher. The irony is, I do not give them any grades. In the certification course however, they are required to get up and teach to demonstrate their ability and understanding of all of the Harada Method principles.

It is vital to learn how to ask questions. I thought sharing some of Girish's questions would be very helpful to you:

1. "What does it mean by Standard Manpower?"

Referring to the Nakamura Chart:

Standard Manpower - Day-to-Day Management - Takashi Harada

Standard Manpower means the ideal number of people you need to get the job done. It means people have the knowledge, experience, and self-reliance and motivation to get the job done well.

Day-to-Day management is the process to develop and open people to their maximum creative ability to work at the ideal state.

2. "Do companies actually apply tools like long-term goal setting form to even front employees like a secretary or workers on shop floor? People may not understand the entire lingo."

Yes, all employees use the long-term goal setting form. It is up to management to explain the new terminology to everyone. It is amazing what people can learn and accomplish with just a little patience and respect from management. The manager might see the workers doing simple repetitive tasks - the work that they gave them - and think that people are not capable of learning new things, but that is not true. Mr. Harada taught under achievers in junior high school and they went on to be winners - they all used the Harada forms. And, he taught thousands of employees, from all levels within organizations, to do the Harada Method.

       3. "How does Mr. Harada in actual organizations turn organizational goals into personal goals?"

      We did this kind of goal setting-workshop in August for one foreign pharmaceutical company in Japan.

       a. The company set a goal of "We want to achieve seven billion yen in 2016," and announced the goal to all of the employees.

       b. Each employee then sets his/her own goal that would contribute to achieving the company's main goal.

       c. Each employee thought of four aspects of goals and purposes: Tangible for them, Tangible for others, Intangible for them and Intangible for others.

       d. Employees shared their goals and purposes with each other and "brushed up" their own goals again.

       e. Each employee delivered his/her own goal to the others.

       f. The employees thought of what they would do specifically to achieve their company's goal and individual goal.

When I run a workshop addressing this question in a company, employees naturally set goals that relate to their work and or their company's goals.

4. "How does Mr. Harada train people in a company. Does he run a workshop for key people who will teach others," etc.?"

There are various ways when Mr. Harada trains people in company. It is completely up to what the company wants and needs. We make separate training plans for each company. We ran a workshop recently for about 600 sophomore employees at one financial service company in August. And we ran also a workshop for one foreign pharmaceutical company in August, but this time the workshop was for all the members of bioscience division.

5. "If the Harada Method is so great, how come the Japanese won so few medals in the London Olympics compared to US and China?"

Only 55,000 people in Japan have had some Harada training. Actually, Japan for its size did very well:

	Gold	Silver	Bronze	Total	Population
U. S.	46	29	29	104	309,975,000
China	38	27	23	88	1,339,190,000
Japan	7	14	17	38	127,380,000
India	0	2	4	6	1,184,639,00

Chapter 25 - An Interview with Jeffrey Liker[38], Author of The Toyota Way

As I mentioned in the beginning of the book, I have had the opportunity to meet and talk to many of the world's best leaders on Lean and manufacturing improvement. Jeffrey Liker is one of those leaders. He has written many books on the subject, the most recent The Toyota Way. Recently, I had the opportunity to sit down with him to talk about the Toyota Production System and the people side of Lean, looking at how it relates to the Harada Method.

BODEK: "Let's talk about the people side of Lean and what you feel are the missing elements to this whole concept of bringing out the best in people?"

LIKER: "First of all, the missing elements have not been missing from the Toyota Production System. They've been missing from people's understanding and interpretation of the Toyota Production System. So, if we go back to Ohno and what he was doing to develop people, there is a direct connection to the Toyota Production System and there is an indirect connection.

---

[38] Dr. Jeffrey Liker is a Professor of Industrial and Operations Engineering at the University of Michigan and the author of: Toyota Culture: The Heart and Soul of the Toyota Way, Toyota Talent: Developing People the Toyota Way, Toyota's Product Development System, The Toyota Way Fieldbook, The Toyota Way and others.

The direct connection is that when Ohno started to move toward one-piece flow, he discovered that inventory caused hidden problems. When problems are not obvious, people tend to ignore them and let them build up. As you "lower the water level" (inventory), as Ohno would put it, you expose the "rocks" (problems), and they become obvious. If you reduce inventory and you know that any problem is going to shut down the next process, you gain a sense of urgency to fix problems very quickly and also to go back and find the root causes and solve them. Otherwise, you'll keep battling the same problems all the time."

BODEK: "How does the Toyota Production System use that sense of urgency?"

LIKER: "The first thing that the Toyota Production System really demands is involvement. If you don't have everybody's involvement, then as you reduce inventory the whole process will just keep shutting down. Shutting the process down poses a challenge to the people doing the work. You have to keep your equipment running. You have to solve quality problems. You have to strive toward perfection, because imperfections will shut down the next process.

When the system is one-piece flow in a sequential process and no inventory, if any of the workers have a problem with the machine or they run out of material, the whole production process is going to stop when they stop. It will be obvious to everybody where the problem is and there will be intense effort to fix the problem."

BODEK: "So a problem in one operation is going to ruin the overall efficiency of the line?"

LIKER: "Right. Let's say there are ten people on the line and everybody is working at a high level of efficiency where they do things right 99% of the time. To figure out the probability of success for the entire line, you multiply the efficiency of each worker by the efficiency of every other worker. With the first two workers, you multiply 99% times 99%. Now you're going to be operating 98% of the time. And then you do that again, and you're operating 97% of the time. If you repeat this for all ten people on the line, soon you're down to about 90% success, even though your line has ten people who each can make a part correctly 99% of the time."

BODEK: "What can you do to make sure the line keeps running?"

LIKER: "The traditional way of dealing with that, if you look at something like Theory of Constraints by Eliyahu Goldratt, is to add inventory. You basically hide the problems and protect the process from the people. What Ohno would do is strip away the protection and put pressure on the people to improve. He wanted them to improve their problem-solving skills and to take responsibility, to make sure that what they do at their process is as close to perfection as possible. So they're responsible for the equipment, they're responsible for communication, they're responsible for noticing that inventory is getting low before it becomes a crisis. Essentially, every person becomes the manager of that process, and they have to solve the problems that occur or they're going to shut down production. <u>That is the direct relationship between the Toyota Production System and developing people.</u>

BODEK: "What is the indirect relationship?"

LIKER: "The part that is not so direct is the way Ohno himself developed people. He would give them challenges, and then be very tough on them and check on them and ask them questions. The people would feel pressured to solve the real problems. Ohno wouldn't go away until they had figured out how to solve the problem, so people felt a sense of urgency to put countermeasures in place and try them very quickly to please Ohno to avoid his wrath.

He basically developed the problem-solving process that we know of today as defining the problem, understanding the root cause, taking countermeasures, checking if the countermeasures work and taking further action when necessary. He didn't write it down because he didn't believe in writing things down, but he was training people by constantly hounding them and checking on them."

BODEK: "It is true, I once asked Ohno to give me things written on the Toyota Production System and he said, 'we do not write things down because things are always changing.'"

Where did Ohno's methods come from?

LIKER: "The type of training Ohno was doing was actually based on the model of the master-apprentice relationship that had never really gone away in Japan. Japan has always been a society that values experienced, senior people who have mastered their skills. It is how the Samurai taught, it is how the great cooks taught, it is how the geisha taught, and it is how you learned the tea ceremony. You train with a strict master, and your job is to please the master. The master gives you assignments, and you don't question them.

You just assume the master has a reason for the assignment and that they are looking out for your welfare, and they care enough about you that they want you to develop you."

BODEK: "It sounds like one of the assignments could be the Ohno Circle."

LIKER: "The Ohno Circle's purpose was really to teach one single skill which was to deeply observe the process and understand the problems. People stay in the circle all day and watch. Ohno would never tell them anything. He would just ask them questions, and they had to more deeply understand the process in order to answer his questions.

Something as menial as standing in a circle for a whole day is a major life lesson - to just get people aware of the importance of deep observation is a fundamental skill of problem solving. That idea spread throughout Toyota into all parts of the company."

BODEK: "In other words, it was important to really master each skill deeply before trying to improve it?"

LIKER: "If you go back to Sakichi Toyoda (the founder of Toyota), he was mastering the loom. His whole life was dedicated to becoming a complete expert and building the perfect automated loom, which he eventually built as the G-type loom. Once he developed it, he retired and then passed on to his son, Kiichiro, the assignment to find something that Kiichiro could do that would benefit society.

Kiichiro selected motorcars. He could have simply bought a knock-down kit[39] (as Nissan did) and assembled cars, but it had been drilled into him by his father that in order to start a project that will benefit society, you have to master every aspect of the technology. So the early workers at Toyota first started by learning how to build an engine from scratch, then they mastered every single element of the manufacturing process of cars, and they cobbled together their own car, which wasn't very good. But they made it themselves from scratch, copying parts of other cars.

That is actually one of the key differentiators between Toyota and Nissan. From the very beginning, Nissan's founders thought they were in business to make cars, and Toyota's founders thought they were master craftsmen dedicating their lives to the art of designing and making cars."

BODEK: "This is amazing. It is all relevant to what I have been involved in these last few years. The Book of Five Rings by Musashi Miyamoto really builds on your message. Miyamoto was a great Samurai warrior back in the 1600s who won 60 battles and never lost. In his book, he speaks to the heart of what you're talking about. It is the real heart. Virtually every Japanese manager has to read this book when he goes through school. It's just brilliant, especially the first part about developing skills and becoming a master.

---

[39] A **knock-down kit** is a kit containing the parts needed to assemble a product. The parts are typically manufactured in one country or region then exported to another country or region for final assembly.

People asked Miyamoto, "How did you win 60 battles and never lose, because every battle is a battle to the death?" He replied, 'I only did two things in my life. One, I polished my sword, and two, I perfected by style. That is all I can do.'

This is a real distinction for you and me. We have to get to what I call quality of work life. We want to build a great car, we want to make great products, we want to have a great work environment and we want to make people great. But we're not there yet."

LIKER: "Right, I agree."

BODEK: "What do you think a great work environment dedicated to developing great people would look like?"

LIKER: "I believe that if you look at Japan, and I think you would find somewhat similar in other Asian cultures, **the culture is really built around the idea of developing people using the master-apprentice relationship.** In Japan, It starts even when you are in kindergarten, where you have somebody in first grade who you look up to take responsibility for teaching and developing you. The students take responsibility for every aspect of operating the classroom from cleaning the floors to preparing lunch.

That was the basis of my book The Toyota Way to Lean Leadership[40] that Gary Convis and I came out with in 2011. The starting point is how you develop leaders. Toyota has a way of developing leaders that really goes

---

[40] Published by McGraw-Hill

back to Ohno's notion that you develop leaders by giving them a challenge and by watching them. Then, through asking questions and making suggestions, you move them toward the Toyota way, which is a set of values."

BODEK: "What are some of Toyota's values?"

LIKER: "The first value is experiencing any challenge as something positive - as something that is giving you an opportunity to get better, to get stronger. Of course, facing a challenge can be stressful, but getting through it can develop each person and increase their confidence and make them more comfortable taking on the next challenge. So quality of work life does not always mean life should be fun and easy. Even the recall crisis, which was horrible for Toyota and cut to the very core of their reputation was ultimately viewed as a challenge for Toyota to improve them self. All leaders at Toyota took on the challenge of learning what they could from that crisis.

Other values in the Toyota Way include respect for people and learning the art of kaizen - the actual process by which you meet the challenge. Teamwork is critical to get different perspectives and identify cross-functional issues. Respect for Toyota starts with putting the customer and society first. There is also genchi genbutsu (go and see), which places a high value on understanding the actual situation very, very deeply before you make assumptions.

In addition, we talk about management by facts as one of Toyota's values. Ohno had a famous quote where he said data is great, but he much prefers facts. Getting the facts is necessary before you can figure out what the problem is and understand its root cause. Once you have the facts, you can find the root cause, then test countermeasures and observe what happens. If you improve the process, you monitor it long enough to see that the process is actually changed. Then you start another improvement cycle.

As you know, the system is based on plan, do, check, act - but at a very deep level. This means you go to the gemba (factory floor), practice kaizen (continuous improvement), set a challenge to move - all at a certain level of inventory, equipment up time, quality, etc. - until you become comfortable. As soon as you have mastered that, then you take on the next challenge."

BODEK: "What role does a leader play in this?"

LIKER: "It is the job of the leader to take responsibility for those challenges without fear of failure, and to learn to coach their people so they will take on those challenges with the humbleness to realize that not every measure they take will work.

That is why Toyota uses the term "countermeasures" and not "solutions," because solution suggests that: 1) you know what the answer is; 2) that there is one answer; and 3), once the answer is in place, the system is fixed. Countermeasure suggests you're going to try something, see what happens and learn from it. Then you're going to try something else and see what happens and learn from that. The learning is continual and you get closer and closer to perfection.

So the elements of the Toyota system are challenge, kaizen, respect, genchi genbutsu, and teamwork.

Teamwork is defined in the Toyota Way as a balance between individual development and team development. **They firmly believe that the best team is made up of great individuals who then work collaboratively**. You don't take a mediocre set of individuals and make them a great team by assessing them or running them through a short training course. **You get an excellent team because you have excellent people who are mastering their craft.** In addition, they respect the knowledge and mastery of others in the team who have different skills, and then they work collaboratively. So these really great, exceptional people work together and when they collaborate, they become an exceptional team. All this is all included in Toyota's concept of teamwork."

BODEK: "How did it work when Toyota first tried to bring this to America?"

LIKER: "They started teaching teamwork back at their joint venture with General Motors, NUMMI. This was their first North American auto plant, and they poured a ton of resources into NUMMI. For every team leader, every group leader, every manager, and every executive, Toyota had a one-on-one coach for years, and executives had one-on-one coaches for their entire careers. The one-on-one coach was acting as a master to the apprentice. The Americans at various points didn't like it very much because they wanted to be free of the Japanese masters. We as Americans like to be independent - we believe we reach a point where we are the experts and we shouldn't have to be taught anymore. However, from the point of view of the Japanese, their job was to help the Americans become excellent and follow the Toyota Way, constantly working to improve.

Toyota did a good job at NUMMI, and they did a good job at the Georgetown, Kentucky plant, particularly in the early stages, when they had one-on-one mentors."

BODEK: "What happens when companies try to copy Toyota?"

LIKER: "When an American company wants to learn the Toyota Production System, the first thing they see are the tools - they see the Andon[41] and they see that equipment up-time is really good, and they learn about preventive maintenance. The Americans want up time like Toyota; they want quality like Toyota; and they want workers who are engaged and making suggestions. They look for the tool that will give them that result. They assume that if you get the right tool in the hands of people who are trained in using the tool, you will get the same result as Toyota, but it doesn't happen."

BODEK: "Why not?"

LIKER: "The reason they don't get the same results because they don't understand that **the tools are primarily there to develop people.** Toyota has been working for decades on developing people, while the copying company hasn't done that. They haven't developed the right culture. They haven't developed people. They don't have people who really want to take on a big challenge because a big challenge is a hassle. They don't have leaders who can coach and develop a

---

[41] Andon is a signboard indicating what part of the plant has a problem. Its up on the ceiling with lights: red light on when the line stops, yellow light when the employee needs help and green indicates everything is fine.

vision of what they can become or understand the means to achieve a vision.

For most people, Lean just becomes another assignment - you know, here are five more things I have to do. I have to put in today's work and write these worksheets and I have to respond to these Andon calls, and it's just a list of additional tasks. They don't see how it is linked to personal mastery. There are very few in the company who really knows this either. In some cases, there might be a few individuals in a company of tens of thousands of people, who understand, but they are frustrated because they are spread so thin.

When the consultants I work with and I are brought in by a company, we explain all of this. We explain that the Toyota Production System and the Toyota Way are really about people development. We explain that it takes time to develop people, that it takes coaches who have the expertise, for example. The managers we are talking to need to have the expertise to solve problems, to improve processes, and to coach the people who work with them. They usually don't have these skills, so they have to get them. We have to coach people to the point where they have some mastery, enough that they can train leaders. Then the leaders can train other leaders, and it becomes a chain reaction. But that takes years."

BODEK: "So where do you start?"

LIKER: "In Toyota's case, when they work with outside companies, their preference is always starting with a model line in one area of the company. Leaders spend enough time there that they develop a minimum level of mastery among the people working in the area and the people that they are training to be coaches."

BODEK: I can see Toyota doing this, but what about other companies?

LIKER: "Usually, the leaders of the companies we work with like the idea of developing great leaders - at least in theory. They like the idea of people mastering their tasks. They like the idea of teaching people and developing people, but they also have enormous pressure to get results - to get results now. The Lean conversion process soon devolves into deploying the tools as quickly as possible, in as many places as possible.

We're going through this process now with a company where the chief operating officer is totally behind us. We agreed that we need to develop the executive leadership team and be committed to a long-term process, at least over several months, of training people in little bits, having them do something and then doing some more training. We are also making an investment in the executive leaders who have to lead this and delegate the responsibility down to the director level.

The problem is the director has cut the whole program from a long-term process of developing leaders to a five-day workshop. Sometimes we'll ask for five days, but it might get cut down to three. Then, after three days in a classroom, the leaders are supposed to be "experts" on how to lead in a Lean way. This means they themselves have to learn the skills of solving problems in a very deep way and then they have to learn how to coach others to solve problems. Of course, after three days they don't have any of the fundamental skills. They haven't even stood in a circle for a day[42], which is the most fundamental skill, and just an absolute baby step. For Ohno, that alone would take one day, but we obviously don't have time to do that. We can show a slide that demonstrates the Ohno Circle, and we can say what it means, and the managers will nod their heads and think they have mastered it.

Too often the idea of mastery is that if we understand the concept intellectually to the point where we can define it, we have mastered it. We just think that if we understand something intellectually, we ought to be able to do it."

BODEK: "Understanding something well is very different from being able to do it well."

LIKER: "Exactly. The Japanese know, as does any good coach, that there is no direct connection between what we understand intellectually and what we have the capacity to do. On the other hand, if we have the capacity to do something, then we will intellectually understand it very deeply. Most of what we understand comes from what we do and how we act. But, you can't get somebody to understand something well enough intellectually and then expect them to automatically perform a task or perform a complex skill at a high level. Try teaching basketball without the student ever touching the ball.

---

[42] Taiichi Ohno would draw a circle in the middle of the factory floor and insist that the plant manager or company president stand in the circle for the entire day and just look for waste.

We have it backwards. I think part of that is the western culture in which we have learned that through science we master the universe by categorizing it and then understanding the relationships between categories.

This mindset leads to things like the Six Sigma[43] methodology, which starts with y equals a function of x. If we want y, which is the outcome, and we figure out what the right x's are, then we can solve the problem. That is completely contrary to what Ohno was teaching, which is that you don't really understand a problem until you deeply observe it. You experiment by trying things, you observe the results of your experiments, and over time you learn."

BODEK: "Our belief that we can control the universe also gives us a much shorter time perspective too. We expect to be successful much quicker here than they do in some countries. For example, many Japanese companies have a 50-year or 100-year plan for their business. In America, we rarely think beyond the next quarter! How do you build a successful company for the long-term if you don't have a long-term plan? Can you talk about the need for a long-term vision?"

LIKER: "One example is Toyota's success with the Prius and other hybrids. What did Toyota do? Eiji Toyoda, in the booming early 1990s, asked, 'Can we survive in the 21st century with the type of R&D that we are doing? ... There is no way that this (booming) situation will last much longer.' So Toyota picked some of the best minds

---

[43] Six Sigma is a very powerful process but Jeffrey is challenging you to think deeper into the purpose of the original cause of the problem.

in the company and explained their purpose was to equip Toyota for the 21st century. They said, 'We haven't changed the way we design or manufacture cars since we started this business, and if we don't adapt, if we don't learn, if we don't change, we will go out of business. So you're really the key to our future.'

A concept team and a prototype team came up with is the first Prius - the first mass-production hybrid. They went through a painstaking process of trying to understand what the 21st century car is going to look like. They assumed it would be environmentally friendly and spacious at the same time, so that is what they wanted from the first Prius.

Toyota spent well over $1 billion in the development process because they believed they had to master all the key technologies themselves. They didn't subcontract out the development and manufacturing of key switching circuits. They developed their own hybrid engine and a new transmission. There were a lot of skills they didn't have. They wanted to make the high-performance batteries, but they realized they couldn't in the time they had, so they partnered with Panasonic. Nevertheless, Toyota owned 51 percent of the joint venture, so they still controlled the technology and they had their people there to master it.

The Prius was the first countermeasure for Toyota. The idea was to get something out in the marketplace they could learn from. The critics looking at it from a western point of view said it was ridiculous. 'They're selling at such a low level,' they said. 'It is such a small percentage of sales, look at how much Toyota has spent, they're losing money on every Prius,' etc. They criticized what

Toyota was doing because that particular vehicle was not profitable given all of the investment costs, even though Toyota never expected it to be profitable. They had no illusions of that. It was simply a countermeasure. It was simply a first step to learn. Toyota wanted to get it out in the market as quickly as possible and then work the bugs out."

BODEK: "They had a long-term vision of where they wanted to be and they stuck with it."

LIKER: "Yes, and then the second generation Prius does better and then the third generation Prius does even better. Toyota then starts to add hybrids to other vehicles, and **every vehicle they come out with is better than the last one, because they are building and learning**. They are not in secret but invisible to most of the public - continuing to master all these individual technologies for the future, like battery technology. They tripled the capacity of the battery while reducing the size by two-thirds, and they improved the process of making the battery to reduce the cost. They also put all that investment into learning. The Prius C (smaller Prius) would not have been possible at prices little more than comparable small cars without this intensive kaizen on the battery."

BODEK: "What about the American car companies? They have hybrids too."

LIKER: "Ford bought Toyota's technology at first. General Motors decided it was too much of a baby step to come out with a hybrid, so they tried to leap frog Toyota with an electric vehicle. They went for the home run in one step, and they ended up with an electric Chevy

Volt, which currently is selling at very low volumes because it is very expensive and you cannot drive very far. They missed the whole point of what kaizen means and the importance of kaizen, the importance of learning, the importance of mastering. Where does GM get its batteries? They buy them from subcontractors.

There is a fundamental philosophical difference in the way Western companies view themselves, their tasks, their people and how to improve processes, all of which is very mechanistic. Western companies think, 'We need to find the independent variable, we need to manipulate it and we will get the result we want.'

This is very different from the learning orientation of a company like Toyota, which is, 'We will have a vision; we will have a specific short-term target for the next step; we will innovate through trial and error to achieve that target.' The target is a challenge, and they believe they will always achieve the target. They're never going to be satisfied, even with 99.9 percent success. It has to be 100 percent success. Then they can move on to the next target, and to the next target after that.

In the process of achieving the targets, employees will be developing themselves. It is hard, hard work. People work long hours, and they are extremely committed to the company. They are also committed to learning and developing themselves, so they can contribute more to the company."

BODEK: "What is the secret to getting people to work so hard and be so committed to developing themselves and to the success of the company? Where does this dedication to improvement come from?"

LIKER: "In the Toyota Way to Lean Leadership," we refer to various eastern religions and philosophies, such as Confucianism. Confucius said that when we're born we're not a human, we're an animal. Our whole life is dedicated to becoming human. As you grow, you go from having a completely selfish orientation to seeing yourself as part of the family and wanting to contribute to the family. Next, you see yourself as a part of a community, wanting to contribute to that community. Ultimately, you want to contribute to society or even to the cosmos. The person who is dedicated to self-development is always trying to impact a bigger and bigger part of the world.

Confucius says that as you become human you have an obligation to teach others and develop others. And also, if others want to become human, they have to seek out teachers. He teaches it is important to respect your elders, your father and people in authority. If they are older and wiser and they have mastered their skills, then you should treat them with the utmost respect and do everything you can to learn from them. He also says you don't have to respect someone older than you or in authority if they don't actually know anything, if they have not mastered their skills.

There is a Japanese version of Confucianism that is very much behind a lot of what we see at Toyota, even though it is not explicit. Buddhism has very similar principles.

So all these eastern religions have a respect for what we can't know, and what we are striving to learn little by little as the world reveals itself to us. They have respect for patience. They have respect for trying to understand the world by attempting things - by actual experience. They have respect for observing deeply with an empty mind.

Ohno would talk about observing deeply with an empty mind, and asking 'why' to every problem five times. That is built on the teachings of eastern religious philosophies."

BODEK: "So you're saying that eastern religion and philosophy have played a big role in Toyota's success?"

LIKER: "I think if you asked Ohno if he learned his method of observing and asking why from Taoism or Buddhism, he would probably say, no, it's just a common sense way to solve problems. But, I think he was directly or indirectly influenced by the way of thinking he grew up with, especially working at a company like Toyota that started with a great innovator such as Sakichi Toyoda."

BODEK: "In any case, Toyota has a long history and culture of innovation."

LIKER: "The whole process of: thinking, taking on a challenge, deeply understanding the problem, trying things and incrementally moving toward a vision, is really the center of the Toyota Way. It's not the tools that you see. It is not having the Andon light. It is not having standardized work posted. That was never really what it was about. Critics say, 'Well, Toyota is really good at incremental improvement and fine-tuning processes, but they're not good at innovation.'

This is a fundamental misunderstanding of innovation. The assumption is that innovation comes to some people suddenly. For example, it's the brilliant idea you might get while you were taking a shower, where you suddenly figure out the answer, and it works when you test it.

But, more often, when you look at people who are excellent at what they do, you find that people actually had to learn a lot of basic skills, through incredible amounts of practice, before they could come up with their brilliant idea. The idea of 10,000 hours of practice has come into our lexicon from Malcolm Gladwell's book, Outliers. Gladwell talks about how people like Bill Gates, Steve Jobs and the Beatles didn't just suddenly become great musicians or great entrepreneurs. In all cases they put in at least 10,000 hours of practice. They developed their skills and mastered their technology or their business or their art. Then, when opportunities arose, they became rich and famous or exceptional in some way.

There seems to be a convergence in thinking between what is coming out of the western literature about the importance of mastery and some of the martial artists who are truly masters of their martial arts and have been writing books about leadership. There is still a fundamental disconnect between what we intellectually think is interesting and what we are willing to do. That comes from a lack of leadership - a lack of leaders who really have the skills, the deep understanding, the dedication to developing other people, and the knowledge of how to do that."

BODEK: "Toyota has been successful developing the right type of leadership, hasn't it?"

LIKER: "The Toyota people got pretty good at doing it in Japan, and they did their best to develop people in other countries, such as America, to continue that process. However, I think at Toyota there was a falloff in the skill-level over time, as the company's leadership passed from generation to generation. Many of the leaders in America don't stay around long enough to really gain the skills. They leave for jobs that pay more money or other opportunities. Toyota works obsessively at trying to get better at developing people, and better at retaining people in other cultures.

There is a basic problem in most companies, but it is not that we don't understand intellectually the importance of developing people. It's not that we don't know the characteristics of a high-performance team. It's not that we need a better cultural survey. **The problem is that we need to develop a culture where we expect to really develop other people**. That element is strong in certain parts of our society."

BODEK: "What parts?"

LIKER: "If you are a musician, and you want to be really good at your musical instrument, you can't depend on school. You have to hire a personal coach, a music teacher who is an excellent performer and who has developed the skills to teach. Your teacher is going to give you drills, and the drills are going to be boring as can be. If you are really serious about performing the instrument, you need to practice hours every day. One third of that practice will be just doing drills to master technique, a third will be learning new music, and a third will be practicing music you've already learned. **People fall down if they don't have a really good coach, a skilled music teacher, or if they don't have a strong passion for the instrument**. They jump to playing the songs that they've already learned, but they don't want to work on the drills and learning new pieces, because that is tasking. It takes a lot of discipline, and it is kind of painful, whereas playing something you already know is kind of fun."

BODEK: "This is wonderful. We're thinking very similarly. Harada has perfected what you have explained to me about developing people.

There is still one area that I am not 100 percent comfortable with, however. It's this distinction between moving towards mastery and the work we give people on the assembly lines. I see people on the assembly line doing the same thing over and over again, and they're not working toward some passion, some mastery. How can a company like Toyota claim they respect people and then give the workers these repetitive tasks?"

LIKER: "Assembly lines are only one part of Toyota. But even in this case, while you do see people doing the same job over and over again, what you don't see is that the Japanese Toyota team member installing five different things in one minute over and over again is actually experiencing a higher level of personal mastery than most engineers in the U.S. are experiencing. Our engineers aren't experiencing any personal mastery. They're just doing their job, and they're doing it the way it has been done before, and they're doing it in the simplest way they can without having to think[44]."

BODEK: "You're saying that the person on the line at Toyota, repeatedly doing the same thing, is moving towards a sense of mastery?"

---

[44] This is a pretty strong statement and I am sure that Jeffrey is just trying to shake up our engineers to think differently on how they design jobs for people.

LIKER: "Yes, in Japan more so than in the United States, because in Japan they have grown up with this culture where you learn skills from the master. They believe that no matter how menial the task appears, there is a lot of skill imbedded in it, and there is a lot to learn. That idea is natural to them, so they do it. Even doing a single one-minute assembly job, they're going to work on mastering that. Things are always changing too. There is more variety in the cars. There are more parts to handle. The workers are looking for quality problems. They are looking at the quality of materials coming in. They're inspecting the work that has been done before them. There are so many things to think about and work on that, overall, most is happy doing that one job."

BODEK: "In other words, a job might look boring to the outsider but there is a lot more happening than you can see from walking past them in the factory. They're not just tightening eight bolts on every car - they're still learning a lot about the manufacturing process, even though it might not be obvious to someone on the outside. What happens when they have mastered their job?"

LIKER: "If they get assigned to be a team leader, which means now they have to lead and teach and develop other people to do a set of jobs, they are happy to take on that role. That is a whole new set of skills to master. Whether they're doing one job or they are leading five jobs and teaching people and doing a bunch of other tasks, the task variety is not as important to them as the depth of learning."

BODEK: "You're giving me a new way to look at something I have been struggling with for a long, long time. Could you explain a bit more how Toyota trains their workers and builds a culture where everyone becomes an expert?"

LIKER: "In general, Toyota has not done as much with what you have described to me with the Harada Method, as far as trying to be expert coaches and developing a specific methodology that is teachable. They have done it, but it has mostly been natural, on-the-job development. And, because they have the culture and the passion, they do it well."

BODEK: "Is it all on-the-job training?"

LIKER: "No, not all of it. About five years ago, probably because of globalization, Toyota introduced Toyota Way training. Toyota recognized that in Japan, the Toyota Way comes more naturally to the workers because when people enter the company, they learn the Toyota Way from day one. Outside of Japan, however, Toyota is hiring people who need more explicit training in Toyota's methods.

Toyota introduced fundamental skills training through their Global Production Center, where trainers teach you by breaking down a task, for example teaching the fundamental skills of caulking a car body. You practice these fundamental skills offline over and over again before you can then go on the line and actually start caulking a body. You learn the fundamental skills by doing drills first.

They developed that training, which was brilliant, but it was missing something. Toyota believes the core of kaizen is the problem-solving method - you learn the problem-solving method, and then you teach it to others. Teaching others the problem-solving method and training them to be coaches is what they call "On-the-Job Development" or OJD. Toyota recognized they did not teach this well, nor did they teach how to be a coach well.

So they gave that assignment to the United States' division, saying 'You're the most mature organization outside of Japan in the Toyota Way, and we, (in Japan), can't figure out how to teach it because it comes so naturally to us that it is hard for us to make it explicit.' They asked the United States' team to develop a training method for teaching people how to be coaches in the Toyota Way."

BODEK: "It took an outside perspective to teach the new methods. What were some of the key things needed to make this happen?"

LIKER: The prerequisite was that U.S. managers had to learn Toyota's Business Practices, (their 8-step problem solving methodology[45]), and Toyota's values[46] and also

---

[45] The 8 Steps consist of: 1 - Clarifying the Problem, 2 - Breaking Down the Problem, 3- Setting a Target, 4 - Root Cause Analysis, 5 - Develop Countermeasures, 6 - Seeing Countermeasures Through, 7 - Monitor process and results, and 8 - Standardizing and Share Successful Practices. In Toyota's culture "Problem-Solving, Everybody-Everyday," means people are empowered to make a difference in their own work areas, contributing to their own job security.

[46] Toyota Values: Engaging Professional Excellence, Welcoming New Challenges, Encouraging Teamwork, Customer First, and Global Perspective

to have some level of mastery on how to solve problems. Because they understood the principles[47] of the Toyota Way and had skills in leading problem solving, the focus was on developing other leaders to lead problem solving while developing others. They start out with a few days of classroom training, mostly role-playing and activity practice, then the leader picks the student they are going to coach on how to use OJD[48] to develop others, and they choose a problem to solve with the student. It may be a little confusing, but it is leaders teaching other leaders to be coaches of OJD.

Leaders pick a problem explicitly to help them improve their coaching skills. If they are at a senior level, the

---

[47] Toyota's Principles: Long-Term Philosophy, create a continuous process flow to bring problems to the surface, use "pull" systems to avoid overproduction, level out the workload (heijunka), build a culture of stopping to fix problems, to get quality right the first time, standardized tasks and processes, use visual control so no problems are hidden, use only reliable, thoroughly tested technology that serves your people and processes, grow leaders who thoroughly understand the work, live the philosophy, and teach it to others, develop exceptional people and teams who follow your company's philosophy, respect your extended network of partners and suppliers by challenging them and helping them improve, go and see for yourself to thoroughly understand the situation (genchi genbutsu), make decisions slowly by consensus, thoroughly considering all options; implement decisions rapidly (nemawashi), become a learning organization through relentless reflection (hansei) and continuous improvement (kaizen)
[48] OJD – on the job development

problems typically take about eight months to solve. During this time, they take a very self-reflective, critical approach to themselves as they coach their student. In addition, the leaders also have a coach who is watching them and giving them feedback. By the end of the eight months, the leaders are much, much better at teaching others how to be mentors of on-the-job development. When one level of leaders has been trained, Toyota moves down the organization to teach the next level the same thing."

BODEK: "How long is it going to take for Toyota to implement this new coaching system throughout the company?"

LIKER: "When I first learned about it, they had been doing this in North America for over four years and they expected it would take a few more years before they get all the way down to the group leaders and team leaders. So, it is roughly a six- to eight-year process, which was also true of Toyota business practices.

This is the first time Toyota has actually had to make explicit[49] the process of coaching, and they're doing the best they can. **Their vision is that every leader in the company across the globe becomes a coach who is developing the people they work with, through actual practice, actual projects and through on-the-job development, which is the most critical way of teaching and developing people**. The classroom is almost irrelevant, but there is some value in telling people

---

[49] Explicit is to fully and clearly express and demonstrate; leaving nothing merely implied.

what the concepts are and giving them a feel as to why they are going to do this. Ninety-nine percent of learning is still on-the-job with a coach. I am interested in learning more about the explicit methods that Harada has developed for teaching this.

BODEK: Thank you so much, this has been great. The more you learn about the Harada Method and Takashi Harada, I am sure you'll get an idea of why this man is considered the best coach in Japan. One of the subtle differences from Toyota is that Harada did it very quickly, very fast. Within two years, he had the first student win the championship medal; eventually he had students win 13 championship medals within five years."

LIKER: "That's what we want, if it is truly effective."

BODEK: "And, we can all get there, if we use the Harada Method. Jeff, thank you so much for your help. Thank you very much."

LIKER: "You're welcome."

Chapter 26 - Interview with Robert Miller, Executive Director of the Shingo Prize

The Shingo Prize is a highly coveted prize within industry that encourages companies and their employees to improve their productivity and quality performance. The Shingo Prize plays a major role in inspiring organizations to be more internationally competitive.[50]

BODEK: "Today, I would like to discuss how the Shingo Prize relates to Toyota's "Respect for People" and the human side of Lean, which is really what the Harada Method is all about. I'm very grateful for the great things you've been doing all these years with the Shingo Prize. You created a major shift in the prize by establishing some very clear principles to help people understand what they should be doing in their organizations to be successful. Where did the shift come from?"

MILLER: "The thing we did is we figured out what Mr. Shingo was trying to teach about people. His thinking on people was not as obvious as his methodologies for zero inventory, Poka-yoke,[51] SMED[52] and all those things.

---

[50] You can find details on how to apply for the Shingo Prize at http://www.shingoprize.org/
[51] Poka-yoke is a mistake proofing process Dr. Shingo created to obtain zero defects.
[52] SMED is Single Minute Exchange of Die a methodology Dr. Shingo developed to force engineers

Those methodologies were crystal clear, since he taught them and wrote about them. But Shingo also had a philosophy, and we had to really work hard to dig in to understand it. We got to the essence of it, and then we correlated his ideas with ideas from a lot of other unconventional thinkers over the last 30 or 40 years."

BODEK: "What did you learn from Shingo's philosophy?"

MILLER: "Shingo said you don't teach people how to do things, nor do you teach people how to focus on people. Rather, you teach people principles. The principles are, as Shingo said, the "why" behind what you are doing. When people understand the reasoning behind what they are asked to do, something clicks inside of them. It is much different than just giving them a bunch of tools, methodologies, or projects. When people really understand the meaning and the deeper concepts, you empower them in an entirely different way.

The whole model of the Shingo Prize has shifted to place an equal emphasis on obtaining results and on bringing out ideal behaviors from people. The ideal behaviors come when people when they understand the principles behind what we're asking them to do. That is an important philosophical shift. I know that you understand this because you knew Shingo better than almost anybody. It took us a lot of time to figure it out. Therefore, what we teach are principles."

BODEK: "Please tell me more about the principles."

---

and managers to find ways to reduce all change-overs to less than ten minutes.

MILLER: "In the Shingo Prize model, some principles are about people, some are about continuous process improvement, some are about enterprise alignment and some are related to results. We grouped them into ten key guiding principles, so they would be easy to understand. These are things that people have known about for as long as I can remember, and I've been doing this for 30 years.

The Shingo Prize Principles of Operational Excellence:[53]

1. Respect every individual
2. Lead with humility
3. Seek perfection
4. Assure quality at the source
5. Flow and pull value
6. Embrace scientific thinking
7. Focus on process
8. Think systemically
9. Create constancy of purpose
10. Create value for the customer

These principles empower the people who understand them. Too often we teach people a tool, and they learn the tool in a specific context without truly understanding why they are using it. But, if they understand why, they can apply it to other situations. They can think about the tool and say, 'You know what? I'm in a whole different

---

[53] From www.shingoprize.org/model-guidelines.html

setting now, and if I do this and this to the tool, I can use it here, because I know what I'm trying to accomplish.'"

BODEK: "You're really building people's skills and capabilities that way."

MILLER: "When people understand the principles, they can adapt, they can modify, they can innovate - and that's what they do. They make the methodology[54] much more powerful than it ever could be if they only used it in the same context where they learned it. That's the powerful part of the human side of Lean. It really enables people to be the very best of who they are."

BODEK: "You've seen this in companies pursuing the Shingo Prize. What about Toyota?"

MILLER: "Toyota does the same thing. Toyota takes a long period of time to teach these principles to their people in the company. Their employees are capable of seeing opportunities, because they understand the principles. They're not just looking for piles of inventory some place. They understand the principle of flow, and when they understand the principle of flow, they can start to think at a higher level. They are not just looking for ten types of waste. They see that anything that interrupts or impedes flow is waste. Management doesn't have to give people a list. They give them the concept and employees figure it out for themselves. They see things way beyond anything we can teach them in a class."

---

[54] Methodology of the principles lets you stand back and get a different perspective of what you are attempting to accomplish.

BODEK: "Tell me about your first principle, "Respect every individual.""

MILLER: "A lot of times, when people write about Toyota, they say "respect the individual," or "respect people," and we say it is a little bit more than that. We have come to understand it as respect for every single person. You want to respect every single person."

BODEK: "I see. This demonstrates that people at all levels are important; no matter what role they have in the company. That sends a powerful message to the workers."

MILLER: "The thing that's really powerful about principles is that they govern the consequences of our choices. There are principles of science, such as, gravity for example. Gravity is a law that's always been there, so when you let go of an object, it falls down every single time. Because you know it's going to do that, you can plan for it, you can anticipate it, you can harness it, and you can use it to do the work.

The same thing is true with a principle like respect for every person or respect for every individual. When you understand the principle, it shapes the outcomes of your behaviors and your interactions with other people. When I treat people with respect, I can almost guarantee what the outcome of that behavior will be.

Think about business. There's almost nothing in business that you can predict that is repeatable or that you can count on. But you can count on principles. You can count on them so when you act a certain way, when you obey or follow the principles, the outcomes will be almost certain. That's certainly true about respect for people. You treat people with respect and you get all they have from them. They want to be part of your company. They want to commit themselves to you. They'll help you get through hard times. They'll dig deeper inside of themselves because they feel respected.

I know that I just want to be respected when I go to work. I want to feel like what I am, who I am and what I can do are valued and respected. When you treat people that way, you get the very best from them."

BODEK: "What's the second principle of the Shingo Prize?"

MILLER: "We call the second principle "lead with humility." That applies for everybody at all levels of the organization - senior managers, middle managers and employees. Humility is a principle that enables learning and change and improvement. If we don't embrace that principle in our lives, we can't change fast enough. We can't learn new things, because we're stuck in the old ways. We have to be willing to say that what I'm doing is okay - it got me where I am, but it's not good enough to get me where I need to go next. That is the mindset of humility.

The first two principles are very closely connected - the way we interact as leaders with people must demonstrate humility. When we demonstrate humility as leaders, the people who we work with and serve and help, they see it and they respect us as leaders. It improves our relationship with them. It's like the grease that makes improvement happen and accelerates it and keeps it moving.

Humility and respect are two principles we call "enablers." These are enabling principles that really turn on the people, turn on the culture, and accelerate the rate at which Lean can be implemented. They are the two most important principles that enable Lean or operational excellence."

BODEK: "This is wonderful. Could you talk a little more about humility? People reading this might equate humility with low self-esteem or weakness."

MILLER: "Humility is not thinking less of yourself. It's thinking less about yourself. If I am humble, I'm not always thinking about my ideas or how I'm the smartest in the room. Humility doesn't mean you're meek or mild or timid. It means that you recognize that greatness comes from us, not from me. And the more of us I can bring to this work, the more likely we are to be successful.

I just spent two days with the leaders at John Deere this week, and we talked about respect and humility and how it would transform their relationship with their bargaining unit employees. If everything leaders did - every policy they had, every communication they had, every decision they made, - was done with complete respect for the people and with a deep sense of humility, it would completely transform the operation.

Humility is about recognizing that we all have the same capability and that it's not about me because of my position or because I've got a college degree. It's about everybody's capabilities. It applies to leaders as they relate to each other and to the people they lead. It applies to the employees as they relate to each other and to their managers.

If I am a humble person, I recognize other people have experience that I don't have. If I am an employee, I recognize my managers have experience that I don't have, and it would be wise for me to listen to them and learn from them. When people in the front of the organization have humility, they're also capable of learning, of changing, and embracing new ideas because they are recognizing the capacity of other people."

BODEK: "There are two things I'm still curious about. One is this whole idea in America about the individual being different from the group. In Japan, there is a group mentality and a team mentality, and we're different in America because we're a group of individuals. That sort of gets in the way of what you're talking about."

MILLER: "My philosophy is that powerful groups are made up of powerful individuals. When I say powerful, I mean they know how to make things happen. They know how to get results. So, if you want a powerful team, you make sure that everybody on the team knows how to get results. Then, when you add humility and respect, you work with your colleagues and your peers in a very different way because you recognize your contribution is not everything. Other people contribute things that you don't have. I think the two mindsets fit together just fine."

BODEK: "The other problem I keep running into is the structure that gets in the way of change. Let's say a person gets very excited at work and they find something new that they want to do. They think it adds real value to the company, so they go to their boss to ask for permission. Ninety-nine percent of the time, the boss will just say no because saying no is easy. Do something different can be threatening.

What you're saying is very, very good, but how do you break through that mentality, that barrier to change? The Japanese call it "bottom up" leadership. They really give people the respect to make decisions, and they give them the opportunity to learn from their mistakes and to learn from their failures. That does not happen here as much."

MILLER: "Those are hard sorts of barriers to overcome and they're cultural problems. They're cultural problems in North America, but they're also cultural within an organization. There are a lot of organizations that can overcome them, but it takes a lot of effort and a really unusual leader. It really takes a great leader to start breaking that down."

BODEK: "How does the Shingo model help company leaders implement change?"

MILLER: "We have two parts to our model. One part is the definition of the principles. The other part of the model is the diamond that has the principles at the top[55]. This is the whole piece about aligning principles, systems and tools. It shows how you can't think your way into a new way of acting. You have to act your way into a new way of thinking.

If I am a leader and I want to change my mindset about saying no to people and create a culture that encourages change, I take the principle at the very top of the diamond

---

[55] To see the diamond, visit http://www.shingoprize.org/model-guidelines.html.

and say, 'Let's give it a try. Let's do a PDCA[56], and change the way we treat people in this situation.' By doing this, we create a little experiment. And then we'll align the systems of the organization in that area to make sure that the employees, the leaders, and the managers are treating each other with respect and doing what you just said that Japanese companies do so well.

We also get the right tools in those systems and measure the results. We look at the cause and effect relationship between the principle and the results.

The only way I know how to change is to just start those experiments - changing to something new, one department at a time. You have to be curious enough to try something, to create an experiment, measure it and study the cause and effect. Then you repeat the process somewhere else. You talk to people, show them what you did and what happened. Even people who don't agree with the change, will have a hard time arguing with the results. Eventually, your mindset starts to change and the mindset of the people in the organization starts to change."

BODEK: "What kind of results do you get?"

MILLER: "In my experience, results are so much better than the old model of control and directive leadership. The improvement is so clear and so obvious that you can't refute it."

---

[56] PDCA is from the Deming wheel, plan, do, check and act.

BODEK: "What you're saying is absolutely wonderful. It's how you really get people on board, and I give you a tremendous amount of credit for that. It's really in alignment with what I am trying to do with the Harada Method. Do you have any stories to share about this type of change?

MILLER: "As I said, I was at John Deere last week working with the general manager in the Large Tractor Division. His team is responsible for the entire tractor manufacturing in North America. The problem they're having right now is that their business is too strong. They're making so much money and they are launching so many new products that they have basically abandoned all their best practices. They are just doing whatever they have to do to get those things out the door, and they're having all kinds of problems. It's like they are back where they were 25 years ago, and they're just sick about it. They don't know quite what happened or what they need to do fix it.

We spent two days trying to diagnose the problem, and it was really powerful. We went out to the gemba and I was with them. I structured a lens they had to look through to see how they got there, and we did that two or three times. By the end of the third time, these people were almost in tears because they could see, for the first time in several years, what was happening."

BODEK: "Once you figured out the problems, what did you do next?"

MILLER: "The general manager said, 'It took us a lot of years to get here. We've just got to work our way out of it, one thing at a time.' We worked at it for two days.

People were tired and kind of overwhelmed, and the general manager told them, 'Let's just start working. Each of us is capable of doing something. Let's all go back and do something different, and then we'll get together in a week and talk more, and eventually lay out a plan.' There were a hundred things that each one of them saw they could do differently.

It started with the leader. It was the leader who was humble enough and wise enough to let people come to their senses about it all. Change happens one person at a time, one group at a time, one department at a time, one company at a time. We're trying to influence the masses, and that's really what the Shingo model is about.

We still look at all the Lean tools and all that stuff, but at the foundation of it all has to be the people. There's a company in Europe that had several of their operations challenge, apply, for the Shingo Prize this year, including the parent company in Austria. The three facilities that challenged all received some level of recognition. One got a bronze, one got a silver, and one received the Shingo Prize. But the parent - the plant where the parent corporation is - didn't get anything. They were really bad, and they have had a really hard time accepting that. They've been angry about it, and they're kind of badmouthing the Shingo Prize in Europe, even though we're trying to help them.

We just keep pushing them and pushing them and saying this is not about us. This is about them. We keep giving them more facts and more data. I'm sure it's going to end up with us going over and walking their facility with them, helping them to see, because they just can't see it."

BODEK: "That's why I say "overcoming managers' resistance to change" is the ninth waste of Lean. Managers stand in the way because their egos are so big they think they could not possibly be the problem.
This interview has been wonderful. What you just said about the people being the foundation for improvement is so true, and it aligns very well with what we are teaching with the Harada Method. We're definitely on the same page. Again, thank you so much.

MILLER: Thank you, Norman.

Chapter 27 - Interview with John Allen,[57] President, Total Systems Development

John Allen co-edited the 500-page Lean Manufacturing: a plant guide and was formerly responsible for all training at Toyota's Georgetown Kentucky facility. I recently talked with Allen about his Lean experience and how he thinks the Harada Method can be used with Hoshin Kanri.

BODEK: "Throughout the book, we have been talking about how the Harada Method brings out the best from people in an organization. Let's extend the discussion to include how we can use the method to strengthen an entire organization. Specifically, I would like to talk about how the Harada Method can be used in conjunction with Hoshin Kanri,[58] because I think there is a natural synergy between the two systems. Could you start by talking about what Hoshin Kanri is?"

---

[58] **Hoshin Kanri** is a method to capture and deploy strategic goals throughout an organization. Also called **policy deployment**, **hoshin planning**, or simply **hoshin**. It is a strategic planning/strategic management methodology based on a concept popularized in Japan by Professor Kaoru Ishikawa in the late 1950s.

ALLEN: Every organization has a set of strategic and tactical goals that are guided by the organization's mission, vision and operating principles. A company creates a strategic plan and an annual plan, (the current year of the longer-term strategic plan), to assist with prioritizing the goals. One process companies use to adopt the goals throughout the organization is called Hoshin Kanri or policy deployment. Hoshin Kanri is both an alignment system and a business system. It fosters alignment by deploying consistent goals throughout an organization and also provides a foundation for performance management."

BODEK: "What makes Hoshin Kanri unique?"

ALLEN: "A mature Hoshin Kanri system has the following characteristics:

- **Hoshin Planning is a system encompassing both control and breakthrough**. Hoshin Kanri is founded on a control system, often called the "daily management system." This control system manages processes throughout the organization by taking frequent measurements, consolidating them, and reporting the results upward in the management chain. The system indicates where the current capabilities fall short of the organization's needs. The needs become important inputs in the selection of the top-priority goals (Hoshin items). Once Hoshin items are chosen, additional resources and attention may be devoted to them.

- **Hoshin Planning connects an organization's long-term vision to the day-to-day activities of

INTERVIEW WITH JOHN ALLEN

supervisors and front-line employees. From the long-term plan flows the annual plan with the priority goals for the coming year. The annual plan is supported by many lower-level plans that are progressively more detailed and more short-term.

∞ **Hoshin Planning is conceived as a PDCA[59] cycle, but with the sequence changed to CAPDCA so that the "check-act" phases come first.** The first phase is a thorough review of the previous year's plans and outcomes. Management completes a thorough analysis of where, how and why the outcomes differed from expectations. Standard quality control techniques, such as the seven QC tools[60], are used to identify the fundamental causes of problems.

∞ **Each plan focuses on process improvement.** Process improvement is a continuous activity, and since gains are cumulative, analyzing the previous year's efforts provides a list of activities that will yield further gains. Analyzing failures reveals the root causes of problems, helping managers find a course of action more likely to succeed the next time. Analyzing successes highlights courses of action that can be reinforced, repeated, and standardized.

---

[59] PDCA is plan, do, check, act – process improvement from Dr. W. Edwards Deming.
[60] Seven QC tools: cause-and-effect or Ishikawa diagrams, check sheet, control chart, histogram, Pareto chart, scatter diagram and stratification.

- ∞ External events completely beyond the control of the organization are also scrutinized in order to determine whether the planning process could have foreseen them. Once the company gathers this information, much of the groundwork for planning is done, and the remaining task is to select and prioritize actions.

- ∞ **The planning and deployment process itself is subject to the same type of thorough review and analysis, so that it can be improved.** This built-in improvement cycle is one of the ways Hoshin Kanri differs from management by objective (MBO).

- ∞ **The process for arriving at corporate goals is participative.** Discussions of performance targets and the means of accomplishing them take place at every level of the organization. The intent is to give everyone the opportunity to provide input before the goals that they will be responsible for are finalized. This process is known as "catchball," named after the game in which a ball is thrown repeatedly from one person to another in a group. When this process is finished, everyone in the organization understands how their own efforts contribute to the organization's goals. No individual or group has goals imposed on them that they do not feel are achievable.

- ∞ **Aspects of the plan (goals and their components, the relationships between them, responsibilities, milestones, etc.) are captured and documented in considerable detail, using formats that are standardized throughout the**

organization. These formats show how senior management's goals are translated into more specific goals at the next level down, and so on.

∞ **The goals include quantified targets and the actions required to achieve them.** No target is adopted unless the means of achieving it have been agreed upon. The targets and the goals are written down using a series of matrices that capture both dimensions of the plan. These matrices also help verify consistency - all targets should be supported by appropriate courses of action, and no course of action should be adopted unless it supports one or more of the targets.

∞ Therefore, the final plan integrates actions that can be pursued to completion and quantified outcomes that should result from these actions.

∞ **When a unit is not meeting its targets, management provides help.** This is not the type of "help" provided in many organizations, where senior management interferes, takes over or reverses local decisions, leaving local management tarnished with blame. Instead, the aim is to gain an understanding of the underlying causes and to deal with them."

BODEK: "How does a company implement Hoshin?"

ALLEN: "A few months before the end of the fiscal year, top management gathers information and analyzes the company's current data. Executives create a set of performance goals for the next year, which must then be deployed throughout the organization. The managers at the next level down look at the goals and determine how they will respond to them. These goals have to be realistic, measurable and actionable. The goals must also challenge the organization to develop the individuals who will implement them.

The subordinates respond by sending a set of goals back to their superiors. Managers review their subordinates' goals to make sure they are understood and that the sum of the proposed improvements meets the organization's goals for improvement. From this launch point, the Hoshin Kanri, or policy deployment, begins."

BODEK: "It sounds as if a mindset shift from the traditional top-down, one-way management is required."

ALLEN: "Yes, perspectives must change in several important ways. Under the new system, management recognizes that the small things done by everyone will out-pace the large done by a few. If I am a manager, my job is to delegate effectively and monitor how well the workers are fulfilling the plan. As an individual contributor, my job is to accomplish my plan. Anything else is a waste."

BODEK: "How did Hoshin develop?"

ALLEN: "Its development is linked with the spread of quality management principles and practices within Japanese industry. The Japanese Union of Scientists and Engineers first introduced these principles in 1950, in a course with Dr. Deming as the guest lecturer. This led to the widespread use of the PDCA cycle (plan-do-check-act) and the "seven quality control tools" for the management of virtually any operation.

The idea of an integrated company-wide management/planning system became popular in Japan during the 1950s and 1960s. Several things heavily influenced this. First, the Deming Prize, established in 1951, called for companies to have a planning system. Second, Peter Ducker's book The Practice of Management, published in Japan in 1954, proposed management by objectives (MBO). Third, General Motors was successful using its divisional system, which was a novel concept at that time. Fourth, Dr. Juran gave many lectures on general management that were very influential in Japan.

Dr. Kaoru Ishikawa and Dr. Yoji Akao also played important roles in the development of Hoshin Planning. Dr. Ishikawa advocated the idea that each worker was the expert on his or her job, so managers should delegate as much responsibility down to the workers as possible. Dr. Akao formalized this concept into a system of forms and processes that aligned a company's goals with workers' daily activities.

By the late 1960s, many Japanese companies had implemented MBO, and a number of leading companies - Bridgestone Tire, Toyota, Komatsu Manufacturing, and Matsushita - had developed their own innovative planning systems that went beyond MBO.

The term "Hoshin Kanri," referring to this new approach, became widely accepted in Japan in the mid-1970s. By the late 1970s, the principles were formalized, and the first books on Hoshin Kanri appeared. The first symposium on Hoshin Kanri was held in Japan in 1981. In 1988, the Japanese Association of Standards published a series of works dealing with Hoshin Kanri practices.

In the USA, a few leading companies, including Hewlett-Packard, Procter & Gamble, Florida Power & Light, Intel and Xerox, implemented their own versions of Hoshin Kanri during the late 1980s.

Various names for this approach have been used in the West, such as "Hoshin Planning," "Management by Planning," and "Policy Deployment." However, none of these terms is in very wide circulation, even in those companies using Hoshin Planning. Employees can still use the system, even if they do not know what it is called."

BODEK: "What is the relationship between Hoshin Kanri and the Harada Method? How can one support the other?"

ALLEN: "Historically, Hoshin Kanri has not been used to help employees accomplish personal and professional milestones. However, companies have discovered it is impossible to achieve superior results without people who are passionate about improving their work.

The Harada Method provides the framework for integrating personal, professional, and organizational goals into business performance. When employees use the Harada Method to guide their growth, in my experience, they act as if they have been "supercharged" and their unleashed energy now feeds the company."

BODEK: "Why is it important to "supercharge" the employees?"

ALLEN: "Any system that does not have employees' full commitment will rise and fall on the personality of the reviewer or of the manager. Employees' commitment grows when their work is based on their own goals and the goals of the organization. This is what the Harada Method provides. It establishes connections between personal goals and organizational goals.

By modifying the goal-setting process to include personal goals for the individual, the organization sends a clear signal that it values the whole person. The individual reciprocates by making a stronger commitment to the organization.

When this commitment is combined with clear career paths and fair compensation practices, employees see work as a place to grow and not as a constraint. Employees feel like they are taken care of and that they can be self-reliant.

Combining Hoshin Kanri and the Harada Method will result in a powerful force for organizational and personal development. Employees will strongly support initiatives that produce results that benefit both the company and themselves."

BODEK: "The decision to implement Hoshin Planning and Harada Method requires a good deal of thought. What should a company consider when deciding to implement both systems side- by-side?"

ALLEN: "Hoshin Planning combined with the Harada Method cannot simply be "installed" in an organization. If you want to apply the two methods to improve your planning system, you need to take into account several considerations. First, organizations must believe that it is important for managers and supervisors to develop the full potential of their employees.

Second, having a working planning and review system is essential from the outset. Introducing continuous improvement involves change, and without planned action and persistent follow-through, inertia will usually maintain the status quo.

Third, a company must be purposeful about re-designing its planning and review system. The new system must be developed from what the company already has. At first the planning system does not need to be complex. Even a rudimentary planning and review system, if diligently applied, can suffice to deploy the start-up phases of an improvement initiative. However, a basic system will not support ambitious long-term business objectives. It is in the later stages of development of the organization that deficiencies in people development will show up."

BODEK: "How long would it take to implement these systems?"

ALLEN: "The time required to develop a mature Hoshin Kanri system is generally three years or more. Improving the annual planning and development system is a slow process.

The implementation process takes time because some concepts of Hoshin Kanri cannot be applied until other elements of continuous improvement and quality management have been learned. For example, in a mature Hoshin Kanri system, plans are based upon a thorough understanding of the organization's current capabilities. This type of information is not available until the organization learns how to analyze current problem areas and their root causes.

Another example is the use of matrices to record targets and to deploy goals to lower levels in the organization. Much of this will seem strange and unwieldy to management teams that do not have experience with some of the seven planning tools."

BODEK: "What is the implementation logic? In other words, why would a company want to implement Hoshin and Harada?"

ALLEN: "Most organizations feel that a goal-planning process is necessary, so management supports such a process. Often, though, they overlook the need to give the same level of attention to a system of personal development. Typically, organizations select a few individuals and give them targeted and specialized personal development in a range of key areas. However, when companies do not develop their employees, they will not be able to improve overall performance as quickly as they would like."

BODEK: "If a company wants to implement a new planning and development system, when should it start?"

ALLEN: "Because it takes a substantial amount of time to develop an effective planning and development system, the system should be implemented as soon as possible. It is better to start working early on a long-term improvement strategy in order have adequate time to implement it in small, easily managed stages.

To achieve a strong and sustained planning and development system, each element must work in concert with the other. The planning system should set the stage for breakthrough organizational goals, and the personal development system should ensure the organization has the personnel prepared to achieve those goals. Having the two systems in place creates balance between organizational achievement and employee self-reliance. This is why Hoshin Kanri and the Harada Method work well together."

BODEK: "When you implement the Harada Method and Hoshin Kanri, what are some things to consider?"

ALLEN: "There are several pieces to the implementation, each one is vital to its overall success.

First, you need to make sure that your planning and development system is designed to help achieve your organization's business goals and the individual goals for self-reliance. Do not just copy another organization's system. You must make sure the system you put in place will fit your culture.

Second, start with the system that exists now and introduce change progressively, in easily assimilated steps.

One of the keys to success is that you teach managers and supervisors to coach and mentor effectively. If your managers are not comfortable with the new system, they will not be willing or able to teach their employees how to use it. It is also important to ensure that users see each change as a step forward, and that each set of changes results in a practical and workable system."

BODEK: "Please talk a little more about mentoring that facilitates the learning process while guiding the mentee's development toward accomplishing the organization's goals.

ALLEN: The interaction that occurs during mentoring is vital. The actual interaction can take several forms, as seen on the chart above.

Mentoring Model

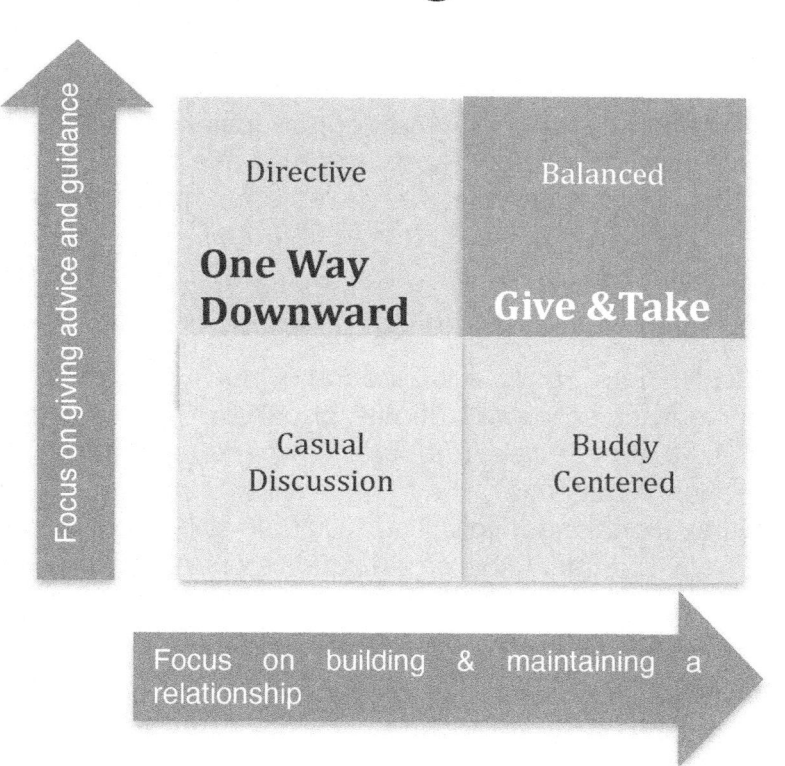

	Directive **One Way Downward**	Balanced **Give & Take**
	Casual Discussion	Buddy Centered

Vertical axis: Focus on giving advice and guidance

Horizontal axis: Focus on building & maintaining a relationship

ALLEN: The interaction that occurs during mentoring is vital. The actual interaction can take several forms, as seen on the chart above.

This model illustrates the situational nature of mentoring. To be an effective mentor you must be able to apply the style of mentoring when the situation calls for it. Establishing a mentoring relationship provides for frank and open conversation that leads the mentee to speak freely about his/her aspirations and dreams.

The mentor must have great listening skills and a willingness to share stories from his/her own life. The mentor must also be supportive and encouraging to the mentee. These conversations allow the mentor to make the mentee aware of what opportunities are available inside the organization and the pathways to reach them. In this way, something as simple as a conversation becomes a very powerful tool for change."

BODEK: "What can a company expect from its integration of Harada and Hoshin Kanri?"

ALLEN: "First, people will become more committed and work harder on organizational priorities. Second, people will take their goals and their own development more seriously because they are now integrated into organizational priorities. Third, people will become more self-reliant. Finally, the organization's overall energy level rises because people come to believe that the organization cares about them personally."

BODEK: "Thank you, John. I appreciate your perspective and insight into a process that can alter the course of an organization."

ALLEN: "My pleasure."

Chapter 28 - Leadership and Lean: Fifteen Questions for Your Lean Journey

> "It is better to lead from behind and to put others in front, especially when you celebrate victory when nice things occur. You take the front line when there is danger. Then people will appreciate your leadership." - Nelson Mandela

The Harada Method can be a key part of implementing and maintaining your company's Lean efforts. It motivates employees and gets them excited about continuous improvement. Where are you and your company on your Lean journey? Below are fifteen questions from expert Lean consultant Shigehiro Nakamura[61] that are useful for determining the progression of your Lean journey:

---

[61] Shigehiro Nakamura is an expert consultant from the Japan Management Association (JMA). His book, The New Standardization: Keystone of Continuous Improvement in Manufacturing, examines various types of standards appropriate to the workplace, how to make them visual for workers and managers, and how to ultimately build them into your machinery and equipment.

1. Do you have an effective method of deploying lessons learned from your organization's successes and failures?

2. Do you have an effective system for making important issues visible and easy-to-understand?

3. What system do you have in place to accelerate cost reduction efforts?

4. Are your company's quality and continual improvement systems at a world-class level?

5. Do you have a system for institutionalizing the results of management audits of your manufacturing systems?

6. Are you using various preventive measures effectively based on your Hoshin Planning System and are you obtaining favorable results?

7. Do you effectively use a one-page business financial report containing a Balance Sheet (BS), Profit and Loss (P&L) and Cash Flow (CF) that is shared with all manufacturing personnel?

8. As an organization, do you set and deploy cost targets throughout the organization as well as require regular progress reports?

9. Do you explain to the organization how costs and delivery performance affect profits and require data from the organization that illustrates their relationship?

LEADERSHIP AND LEAN: FIFTEEN QUESTIONS

10. Do you have a system in place to model and document the skills and techniques of highly-skilled workers?

11. What systems do you have in place to promote continuous and life-long learning of your younger employees?

12. Do you have a system in place for the smooth and rapid transfer of skills and techniques from highly-skilled workers to potential successors?

13. What groundwork are you laying to prepare managers in the event of reabsorbing outsourced manufacturing to shorten delivery times?

14. Are you satisfied with your company's performance in the areas of JIT/SCM[62] and new product development?

15. How do you measure the performance of your new product development process?

As you look at the above list, ask yourself how you can use the Harada Method to establish corporate goals and get everyone aligned in obtaining them.

---

[62] JIT/SCM – just-in-time and supply chain management

Chapter 29 - If You Want to Be Lean, You Need Lean Leaders

"As we look ahead into the next century, leaders will be those who empower others." – Bill Gates

To build a Lean company, you need to have people who want to be the very best in what they do. You need an environment where people work hard and do not live in fear of losing their jobs. Continuous improvement means improvement every day, not just when you get around to it. Choose to be a leader by setting the example and challenging others around you to also become leaders.

Quality of Leaders

You have already learned the history of the Harada Method, and the unique qualities of self-reliant people who contribute to the development of society and their own future. Now, it's time to learn the necessary qualities of leaders who can develop self-directed people.

Leaders can be managers, coaches, teachers, captains, directors or anyone else who have people depending on them for some type of guidance.

Leaders Change Themselves First

What is the most important quality of a leader of an organization? Some say it is to have good communication skills, others say it is management skills, a sense of responsibility, or judgment, or the ability to make decisions.

Self-transformation means **"Change yourself first before trying to change others."** If you want to make your employee be a self-reliant person, the first thing you have to do is to try to be a self-reliant person yourself. Otherwise your employees will never be able to see the true value of being self-reliant. The truth is that what employees do is exactly what leaders do.

Ritsuo Shingo, the former president of Toyota in China and son of Dr. Shigeo Shingo, is an example of this type of leadership. He served most recently as the president of Toyota's Research Center in China, reporting directly to Mr. Toyoda the president of Toyota. A year ago, he keynoted the Shingo Prize Conference and told a story about when he was president of Toyota, China:

"Watch My Tail"

"When I opened the office in China, I needed a car and furniture: a desk, chairs, etc. Instead of going to a store that sold new desks, I went to a used furniture store and carefully selected the items that I needed. I also went and bought a used Toyota. I was not told by my boss to save money, but I wanted to set an example of being conservative to my associates. Since we were starting a new venture in China, I wanted to spend as little money as possible. I did not tell my associates exactly to do what I was doing, but I did tell them to 'watch my tail.'"

IF YOU WANT TO BE LEAN, YOU NEED LEAN LEADERS

Ritsuo wanted to set the example. That is the Toyota Way - where every leader has the knowledge and skill to apply the Toyota philosophy.

You can be a suitable role model for your employees if you work on your own goals. By being a role model, you will offer your employees a good and positive atmosphere to work, making your workplace more active, energetic, and a more productive.

The ultimate purpose of transforming yourself is to change others. Leaders have to be self-transformative because they have to lead the change in their workplace and organization. Therefore, the most important quality for you as a leader is to transform yourself by behaving as a role model for your employees and showing them how to act as self-reliant people.

Chapter 30 - The Difference Between a Leader and an (Old-Thinking) Manager

> *"An employee's motivation is a direct result of the sum of interactions with his or her manager."* - Bob Nelson

A few years ago, I wrote an article for Manufacturing Engineering Magazine on the difference between a Leader and a Manager. It is appropriate to make it part of this Harada Method book, because more than anyone I know, Harada shows us how to become great leaders.[63]

Virtually every manufacturing company in America is attempting to implement Lean principles, but aside from Toyota or their major Japanese suppliers, what companies can claim to be truly Lean? If you know of any, please let me know.

I was recently asked, "How do you sustain continuous improvement to attain Lean initiatives?" I suddenly realized that the question was an oxymoron (a combination of incongruous or contradictory terms). "Sustain" means to continue something that you have done in the past, while "continuous improvement" explicitly indicates constant change. The two represent the past versus the future. It also came to me that the main reason companies are unable to successfully

---

[63] We can become great leaders when we help our employees to become self-reliant and successful in life.

implement Lean comes down to the difference between leading and managing. Very simply, you manage the "past" and you lead change for the "future." Lean needs leaders!

The dictionary is not that helpful when you seek a definition of the words "leader" and "manager," but one appropriate definition of manager from my dictionary is: "a person who controls and manipulates resources." A manager looks at the past to determine how to do things in the future, while a leader creates a vision of what is possible and builds a new future. A manager likes to make decisions based on historical accounting data, with the thought that what worked in the past should work in the future. The leader looks at what is happening now, knows that the future can be much different, and carefully plans for the future.

Traditional managers have been taught to work through layers of subordinate managers. When a senior manager is presented with a problem, he/she discusses it with the subordinate and then normally tells them to take care of it and report back. But in a Lean system, leaders are encouraged to learn for themselves. This approach might be called "management by walking around." The late, great Taiichi Ohno, co-inventor of the Toyota Production System and former VP of Manufacturing for Toyota, would draw a circle on the middle of the factory floor, and insist the senior executive stand in the circle for a day to learn how to truly see operations. He insisted that leaders "wash their hands at least three times a day" to make sure that they would get their hands dirty working in the factory. He also insisted that the senior manager's office be right in the middle of the factory, for he wanted the "power" to be where it was needed; when it was needed.

Do you want to be Lean? Then you must lead Lean on a daily basis. Remember, the manager is often caught in the past while the leader is watching the now and planning for the future. Not long ago, you could walk through most factories and see virtually nothing on the walls. In a Toyota factory, the walls are filled with charts, pictures, sayings - hundreds of constant reminders to workers that tell them how to continuously improve. The famous Andon[64] system, with lights on the ceiling, is designed to share information about the status of production: every worker knows if the plant is ahead of or behind schedule, and also knows when anyone in the plant is in trouble and needs help.

Leadership Versus Management

Below is a chart that compares a leader to a traditional manager:

Leader	Manager
Asks people to learn how to do it	Tells people what and how to do it
Listens and learns from employees	Often doesn't listen
Develops people	Does not focus on developing people - creates an atmosphere of fear
Praises people	Rarely, if ever, praises, easy to criticize them
Gets to know employees personally	Sees only a crowd of workers

---

[64] Andon is a signboard high up near the ceiling inside a factory that shows lights indicating which areas are having trouble and might need help.

Walks the floor (with the troops)	Rarely seen on the floor - most time is spent in meetings
Leaders care for people	Stays detached
Passion for their job	Work is a way to make a living - paid to do it
Uses checklists	Rarely uses checklists[65]
Is a change maker	Resists change
Fights for their employees	Looks to get rid of people
Builds the business from within	Wants to outsource
Keeps workers happy	Unconcerned - they are paid to do their job
Empowers people to make decisions	Maintains power and makes all decisions
Open door policy	Hard to reach
Personable	Competitive with subordinates
Overcomes resistance	Doesn't understand resistance
Genuine	Often insincere
Is not afraid of chaos	Likes order; keep things just the way they were
Goal - let them do it	Distrusting, maintains control
Encourages workers to identify, share and solve problems	Workers hide problems - fear of retribution
Encourages people to grow - rotates workers often	Doesn't care if people do the same job every day
Encourages workers to submit and implement small improvement ideas	Does not give workers a vehicle to offer and implement many little suggestions
Helps people establish annual growth plans	No growth plans for people
Leads by doing	Does not set an example
Delegates authority	Authoritarian but also scared to make decisions
Develop leaders, people that can be better than them	Doesn't care - restrains people from growing, wants followers
Respects people	Does not respect people - looks down at them

---

[65] A pilot, an airplane mechanic, and a good doctor will not just leave it to their mind to remember but will use checklists to insure accuracy.

THE DIFFERENCE BETWEEN A LEADER AND A MANAGER

Easy to ask for forgiveness from	Must ask for permission from
Tries to say "yes"	Quick to say "no"
Risk taking	Avoids risk
Open to new ideas	Closed to new ideas
Often breaks rules	Makes rules for others to follow
Allows failure - allows people to make and learn from their mistakes	People are afraid to make mistakes
Feels good about their job	Not that happy with their job
Sets challenging but reasonable goals	Sets unreasonable goals or none at all
Is excited about their job and people	Lackluster - doesn't feel that good about their job
Focuses on how to make the place better for people	Is not concerned about making the place better for people
People stay and work for them - very low turnover	People anxious to find another boss to work for - high turnover
You work with a leader	You work for a manager
Wants work to be fun	Most people dread the job
Wants productivity, quality, profits and happy people	Wants production, profits and to please their boss
Sets the vision and lets people do it	Directs and dominates what is to be done
Leads people - focus is to grow the company	Leads machines – focus is to cut costs
Shares knowledge	Protects and doesn't really share knowledge
Overcomes past prejudices	Unaware of their prejudices
Inspires	Commands
Has wisdom and continually learns from people around them	Knows it all
On the front line	In his/her office
Loves to see what is happening now.	Loves to look at accounting data
Creates a continuous learning organization	People are stagnant
Develops and supports teams	Keeps workers isolated, easier to control
Looks at flow and removes the obstacles	Looks at production figures and doesn't really understand flow
A coach	The boss

Appendix 1

Spotlight – Five Ways to Build Your Mind

To build your mind means to train your mind to be strong and positive. Some people presume that to build your mind requires the psychological skill training done by many professional and Olympic athletes. The training teaches them to play their sport calmly, which allows them to exercise properly and deliver their best performances at the critical moment.

The five ways are the culmination of what Mr. Harada taught as a junior high school coach. Using the five ways, you can build your mind up to be strong and tough.

1. Use Your Mind - Think and Write

Writing is integral to the Harada Method. You can use writing as an instrument for your improvement. Writing unleashes the creativity within you and is the best way to think deeply and clearly. One of the first steps of the method is to write your Harada Long-Term Goal Form, to define your important goals to be successful in life. (You will learn more about the Long-Term Goal Form in Chapter 4.)

As you write on your Long-Term Goal Form, many things clearly appear: a sense of purpose, affects to others, tips for success, your worst habits that continually fail you, and presumable problems and their solutions. By looking both at your successes and failures in the past, you make it possible to visualize your image of a future success more clearly and concretely.

When I was young, I couldn't write. My teachers told me I couldn't write. I believed them and my grades in English were always low. For years I knew that I was a terrible writer, yet somehow, miraculously, in spite of my limitations, I kept finding the world's greatest management geniuses, and I wanted to write about them. I made myself sit down and write and write, and, overtime, I found that I was really writing – I hope you agree.

Someone who writes regularly also thinks regularly. Stop and take a moment to write down what you are feeling about this book. What ideas from the book can you use to make your life better? Use your mind to think positively to be more aware of what is happening around you.

This is the way it goes - you write, you write more, you write much more, you think deeply, ideas pop into your head, you realize new things, you understand yourself, you stop making the same mistakes and you move closer to your goal, closer to your success.

There is a distinction between using your mind and the mind using you. Dont let your mind control you. One moment the mind tells you that you are happy and the next moment it tells you that you are sad. Harada is teaching you to use your mind for your advantage. With practice, you can control your mind. You can learn how to ignore the negative thoughts that might come. When the mind starts to go in a negative direction, I like to say "cancel, cancel" to break the negative thought pattern.

2. Clean Your Mind - Develop a Feeling of Gratitude

To clean your mind means to develop a feeling of gratitude and a decent, humble attitude. Serving others through cleanup activities or volunteer works is the best way to clean your mind.

In Japan juveniles who committed crimes are assigned to work in programs where they care for elderly people in nursing homes. This type of program teaches the offenders about responsibility, affection and gratitude. The youth are transformed by their interaction with their elders. The people in the nursing home are very grateful for the care and attention, and they repeatedly thank the juveniles. The simple act of saying thank you means much to the young offenders, who have rarely been shown gratitude in their lives.

Through jobs that require responsibility, people feel pride, affection, and gratitude. Simple acts like saying thank you have a way of cleaning peoples minds. Just being open and honest with people can revitalize and help develop them to their fullest.

3. Strengthening Your Heart

In the context of the Harada Method, heart refers to the determination to succeed. You have to strongly believe in yourself. You must feel it deeply. Many people think that the only way to strengthen your heart is by challenging and overcoming some hardship. In reality, perseverance is what strengthens you. Continuously improving something every day without taking a break is what strengthens your heart.

At one of the national track competitions, I remember one final event where a student won by just one inch over his opponent. I still remember that glorious moment when my student smiled and waved at me from the podium, letting me know that he had won and appreciated my small part in his win. He called out my name in gratitude and then I went over and we shook hands. Looking back, I would not say that winning the tournament strengthened his heart. Instead, I'd say that because his heart grew strong, he was able to win. Winning the tournament is a result. It was in the process that his heart got strengthened."

"If I Have One Enemy it is Surely my Ego."

It is not easy to change your heart about things but it is worth the effort. I had a teacher once that said, "I want to be the hero of my own life." I like that phrase and I am willing to do virtually anything to attain that goal. Look at what you are currently doing at work and ask yourself, "what does being a hero mean to you?" Are you the hero of your own life; are you doing exactly what you really want to do and if not, how do you plan to get there?

4. Organizing Your Heart

Organizing your heart means that you begin to view yourself from a third person's perspective. We need to separate ourselves from our past mistakes and failures in order to give ourselves the power to succeed in the future. A failure can give us a strong negative image that persistently sticks in our mind. You may have had a past bitter experience such as failing in a presentation with your client and losing a big account. The more serious you are, the more you think about the failure. You then blame yourself, become depressed and continue to live with a feeling of regret. If you don't deal with the image of that failure, it will appear and inhibit you during your next presentation opportunity. As a result, you wont be able to perform at your best.

I watched small parts of the 2012 Masters Golf Tournament and, like many people, I was interested in how Tiger Woods was doing. At one time, he was the best athlete in the world and today, after his emotional problems, he is no longer as consistent. During the Masters, I noticed when Tiger missed a stroke he was furious with himself. In the past, he was like a Sumo wrestler who is taught to always keep his composure no matter how many battles he lost, but Tiger during the Masters after he missed the stroke would get so down on himself that he just went on getting one bogey after another. I am sure Tiger still has the skill to consistently be the best golfer in the world, but he has to work on his heart and mind (By the way, if you know Tiger, tell him to take my Harada workshop and we will surely get him back to his top form).

Making Mistakes is How We Learn

We must learn to deal with mistakes better, starting at an early age. When you went to school, you took tests and when you made a mistake your grade went down. It is ironic that you go to school to learn, but the system can kill the learning process. How do you really learn? You learn from your mistakes, but schools penalize you for making mistakes. In other words, the school system is telling you, "Come to school but don't learn!"

In actuality, you should be rewarded every time you make a mistake, for it gives you an opportunity to learn. Watch a baby learning to stand for the first time and watch how many times she falls until her muscle system learns to balance. When she finally learns how to stand, she no longer has to think about it, she just does it.

To succeed in this highly competitive world we must get rid of the fear in the workplace.[66] We want to do everything possible to bring out peoples creativity and we must let them learn from their mistakes. You should still exercise care so that the mistakes will be small, but you can learn from your mistakes and then be careful not to repeat them.

---

[66] W. Edwards Deming is famous for teaching Japan fundamental principles of statistics and quality and for his Deming Quality Wheel (Plan-Do-Check-Act) and his 14 Key Principles. Principle number 8 is "Drive out fear, so that everyone may work effectively for the company."

To me, banks are very funny with their systems to prevent tellers from making mistakes. The banks put in expensive systems to catch tellers who can lose a few dollars, while some of their top people have lost billions on the subprime mortgages without any repercussions. It is ironic to put such great pressure on the bank tellers not to make small mistakes that maybe can lose $100 while their traders can lose billions.

Even if you have failed in the past, you can face new opportunities calmly knowing what you can and cannot do. You cannot remove old failures but you can stop regretting them. It is possible to not make the same mistake twice, so think only about the future. Focus only on what you can do now.

What helps you distinguish the past from the future is journaling, writing and planning. Journaling directs you to the future by allowing you to reflect on each day and write out your thoughts and emotions so you can remember what you did wrong and what you can do better in the future. When people know what and why they did something they can now put in their best efforts to establish a new path to take.

5. Expand Your Heart

If you use the Harada Method, you can achieve, with high certainty, what you set as your goals. **What is uniquely different about the Harada Method is that it is like a science. You follow the steps precisely and you will succeed.** If you believe deeply in yourself and set real, meaningful goals, the Harada Method will give you the framework to reach them.

Expanding your heart means becoming thankful for what you have. To expand your heart, you take actions to thank your colleagues, bosses, and everyone else around you through your words and attitude. If a person says that he accomplished everything all by himself, he is just selfish and a narrow-minded person. He misunderstands thinking that self-reliance means that he can do everything by himself. Self-reliance means you can make proper decisions on your own, but you also remember your place in a much greater society.

As a junior high school coach, Harada wanted each student to be a winner and he wanted the school to be the best. For the school to be the best required effort by the students to work for the common good. Although not every student could win a gold medal, he still wanted the students to work towards building a winning team where everyone could share in the victory.

An Individual Skill Becomes a Corporate Skill, Which Leads the Company to be More Effective.

Another way of expanding your heart is to share your wisdom, tools and knowledge with other departments and organizations. A great team builds up a great firm. In Japan this is called, "one plus one equals three." If team members share their strengths with one another, the organizational power and outcome increase beyond the simple sum of each individuals talents.

It is generally believed that the strength of Japan is cooperation. However, I believe the secret of the strength of Japan lies in how to strengthen each individual in a team-setting and to enhance a cooperating spirit.

The five ways of building up the mind, which Mr. Harada formalized during his teaching experience at school, is now used not only by schools but by firms everywhere in Japan. Its purpose is to help people improve themselves by taking initiative in thinking, attitude and action, so that they can use their existing tools and skills correctly. Even though there are wonderful methods, systems and tools, it is only human beings who can put them into practice. The five ways gives people the strength and confidence to do their best.

The tools of the Harada Method should allow you to reach your goals very quickly. As you enlarge your mind, you are going to expand your abilities for your own benefit and for the benefit of others. As you grow and succeed, you will have more talent to use and share. Cultivating the spirit of "jiri-soku-rita" (means my benefit is equal to your benefit) is one of the main goals that the Harada Method is aiming for. It is vital for your personal success to learn how to serve others.

Change

For the Harada Method to work, you must be open to making changes in your own life. This is a challenge. We are all locked in patterns and each day we tend to do what we did before. Some of the patterns are very pleasant, so we want to repeat them, yet some are harmful but we still continue to do them. Why?

In February 2012, I spoke to an APICS chapter in Portland, Oregon. During the talk, I threw the slide clicker into the air and it bounced and landed on the table. I asked the audience, "Why did the clicker fall down? Why didn't it fly up into the air?" They responded, "Gravity, of course." Even though you cannot see it, gravity is a force on this earth that pulls objects toward each other. In this case, the clicker was pulled to the ground.

I then asked them, "What force prevents you from changing?" After a few guesses, we came to agreement that "resistance" prevents us from changing. We seem to be controlled by forces beyond our will. I want you to start to recognize when you see wonderful opportunities to change, how resistance quickly comes up to stop you.

Lately when I keynote a conference at the end of my talk, I ask everyone to get up and raise their right hand and make a pledge that they will go back and do something new that they learned from my talk - especially go back to their place of business and empower all of their employees to start doing the Harada Method. Everyone makes the pledge, gives me a round of applause, and then goes back to their place of business and almost all of them then do exactly what they were doing before.

We say we want to change but it rarely happens unless we are forced to do it. Now, Harada is giving you a new powerful methodology to make a real commitment to yourself to find something in life that you want to be successful at and work out the specific plans to get there. Here is the method to help you make meaningful change.

You are now challenged. What can you do? The first step is deciding you want to change. I can't do that for you. But, once you start to believe in yourself, and you figure out what you need to do to change, by using the Harada Method you can start to change. The Harada Method helps you to make those changes.

Remember when you read in a book or heard a lecture about a new and wonderful management technique. You got excited and really wanted to experiment with it, but you didn't. The mind starts to find many reasons why you shouldn't try it. You mention the new idea to your boss, but believe me the boss is as "stuck" as you are. I asked a top manager in one of my classes, "What do you say to an employee that gets all excited about the Harada Method and wants to go the workshop?" He said, "I immediately ask him or her if the money is in the budget."

What a wonderful excuse! Of course it is not in the budget. The workshop is new, and so many companies relegate the education of their people to the bottom of the pile.

Another reason we resist change is that we fear making a mistake. We think, "We got by yesterday, so why muddy the waters today?" Well, if we really want to succeed in this highly competitive world then we must find ways to overcome our resistance and find new and better ways of doing things.

Appendix 2

PCDSS - A Five-Step Management Cycle for Success

> "Oh, what a world of profit and delight, of power, of honor, and omnipotence, is promised to the studious artisan."
> - Christopher Marlowe, the Tragical History of Doctor Faustus

The Harada Method was developed in the field of education and is now widely accepted and used in many companies in Japan. There are many tools and systems in the world that can produce tremendous results, but it is people who control and put them into action. We must improve people's way of thinking in order for them to be able to operate the tools and systems in the right way and for the right purposes.

To help people manage their minds, Mr. Harada developed the PCDSS management cycle. PCDSS is an expansion and redirection of Dr. Deming's famous PDCA[67] wheel. The difference is that the Deming wheel is normally used for corporate problems while the PCDSS focuses on advancing the competency of individuals, which in turn enhances the strength of the organization.

---

[67] The Deming Wheel: plan, do, check, and act

The five steps of PCDSS are:

Plan - Think and Write

Check - Check Yourself to See if You are Ready

Do - Work Consistently

See - Control Yourself

Share - Help Others

The PCDSS cycle helps you improve your skills for work and for your life itself. In every aspect of life, you set goals, make plans, check your attitude and work consistently, make use of every moment, and go for the goals that benefit both you and others. A person who does this is a self-reliant person.

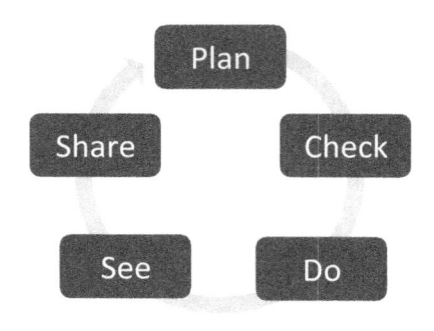

Plan - Think and Write

Plan means to set goals and to write down a date when you want to complete them. The goals you set should be objective, concrete and challenging. The more tangible and measurable they are, the better. Use the Harada Long-Term Goal Form to plan your vision of your future and how you will reach your goals.

Check - Monitor Your Attitude Daily

Having a positive attitude and keeping your mind set strongly on your goals has a big affect on whether you will achieve your goals or not. To create a positive mental attitude, you start by cleaning your home or workplace. By making a daily effort to clean and serve others, you set the right tone for achieving your goals. The positive attitude spreads from you to others. Every day you should check to make sure you are staying positive. If not, repeat your affirmations or talk to one of your supporters.

Do - Work Consistently

"Do" is to repeatedly perform actions that moves you toward your goals, no matter what happens. You might sometimes feel like you are tested by some divine being or fate itself in the process of pursuing your goals. Endurance is essential in times like this. Use the Harada Routine Check sheet as a powerful tool to cultivate your endurance and patience.

See - Control Yourself and Marshal Your Thoughts

In the process of writing your Harada Diary, you will realize what is helpful and what is unhelpful for pursuing success. By reflecting, you will be able to adjust your daily actions. Doing the Harada Diary every day, enables you to "see" what is good for you and what is bad for you. Additionally, you will realize how to make your life better (kaizen) by writing down your past failures. The act of daily reflection and writing in your diary will help you to not make the same mistakes again.

Share - Help Others by Sharing Your Ideas and Experiences

As you change and grow in pursuit of your goals, you want to share your experiences and new knowledge with others in your organization. Through sharing, the organization becomes stronger and more powerful. Each worker's new competencies adds to the total capabilities of the organization.

PCDSS Improves the Whole You

The PCDSS cycle helps you improve by getting you to look at your actions, prepare your mind, and reflect on your progress. You then share your results with other people and grow the knowledge and skills of your organization. By following the PCDSS cycle, your job performance will improve, as will your character.

Enhance Four Aspects of the "Self" to Gain Valuable Confidence

When you write the Harada Diary, you will focus on four aspects of your "self": **self-awareness, self-control**, **self-esteem** and **self-image**.

Self-awareness

You analyze yourself by writing the Harada Diary. Using the Diary, you develop a better understanding of what motivates you, how you work best, and how you can overcome the obstacles that stand in the way of your success.

Self-control

Self control is the ability to apply your awareness to your daily actions. You repeatedly and consciously repeat behaviors that will lead you closer to your goal, while you avoid behaviors that will impede your progress.

Self-esteem

Self-esteem comes from two sources: competence and self-respect. Competence is your ability to perform tasks related to your job. As you improve your skills and increase your competence, you will see yourself as being good at the job and believe you can be even better.

Self-respect is a feeling that enhances your humanity and character. When you act with integrity, you build your self-respect.

Self-Image

Self-image is the image you have of yourself at this moment. As your self-image improves, you gain more confidence. Eventually, you become unquestioningly confident in your ability to reach your goals. Having confidence and a good self-image are essential to achieving your goals in life.

Using the Harada Daily Diary every day will improve each of these four aspects. It will improve your self-awareness, yourself-control, your self-esteem and your self-image.

Appendix 3

"Never, never, never give up."
- Winston Churchill

Six Features of a Self-Reliant Person:

According to the Harada Method, there are six features that self-reliant people have in common. Self-reliant people:

1. **Are open-minded about advice or criticism**

2. **Take responsibility for achieving their goals**

3. **Believe they can win**

4. **Create good habits**

5. **Are effective thinkers**

6. **Are able to live in harmony with the four aspects: spirit, skill, physical condition and a daily life**

Here is a more in depth look at each one of these characteristics:

1. Self-Reliant People are Open-Minded about Advice or Criticism

Picture an empty glass. If the glass is on the table right side up, it is easy to fill the glass with water. If the glass is upside down, though, the water will just spill on to the table.

Think of the glass as your mind, and the water as outside information, such as advice or criticism. If your mind is open, as with the first glass, it accepts the information and uses it to improve. Conversely, if your mind is more like the upside down glass, closed off to new ideas, you will miss many opportunities to improve.

The metaphor of a glass and water demonstrates a key difference between a self-reliant person and a non-self-reliant person. Self-reliant people willingly take advice. They listen to suggestions even if they are not exactly what they would always like to hear. They continuously learn new knowledge, and are willing to try at least one "drink" from whatever is poured into the glass.

On the other hand, non-self-reliant people will not accept suggestions willingly. They lock themselves in a tiny little room where they refuse to engage the outside world. With this mindset, they often cannot make improvements or changes.

Self-reliant people are also open-minded about communicating with others. They say positive things in order to encourage both themselves and the people around them. The non-self-reliant are closed-minded and sometimes treat others poorly. They say negative things that discourage both themselves and people around them.

Question: Should a Self-Reliant Person Listen to Unreasonable Criticism?

Self-reliant people are always open-minded, so they willingly try to communicate with people through difficult situations and even when criticism is unwarranted. This attitude is applicable even for unreasonable claims, strange accusations or even absurd criticism.

Accepting criticism is not easy. Criticism attacks your ego. If you can try to realize that the ego is really your enemy, as it is a false image of yourself, then you can accept criticism as an opportunity to learn something new.

2. Self-Reliant People Take Responsibility for Achieving Their Goals

A self-reliant person thinks like this, "I am the person who is responsible for what I do."

If they are required to sell $25,000 of products each month, they regard the amount as a goal that they want to accomplish. They do not think of the amount as what the manager told them to achieve. The amount is never a quota. It is always their own goal that has value to them as if they had set it themself.

If they do not achieve their goal, they only blame themself—not their manager, not tough times in the industry, not others only themself. They think that they could do much more to make things work out better and they find some new ways to improve for the next time. A self-reliant person tries to change themself first, and tries not to whine about misfortunes or blaming someone else.

The self-reliant person embraces a failure as an opportunity to improve, saying something such as:

> "I should have checked who the person in charge would be in advance, so I could have prepared more."
>
> "I could have made my presentation shorter and better."
>
> "I should have asked them to attend the meeting with several people and not just one person."
>
> "Here is what I am going to do. I will try much harder to be trusted as a strong salesperson in the industry. I will call the manager directly next week to get an appointment for another sales presentation."

Someone with this attitude never feels like a victim. They believe they will find a way to take advantage of the next opportunity. They believe the situation is changeable if they are more creative and perseverant.

I once had the idea that I could help Macy's improve their customer service, and I was determined to reach the President. I called Macy's and asked the first customer service representative for the telephone number of the President or at least to give me the address where he was located. The operator did not know the name of her President and did not know his address. I then asked for her supervisor, who also did not know either the name or the address. But, undaunted, I carried on the game and kept asking for each person's supervisor to talk to. I was persistent, and after 20 calls, I finally reached the secretary of Macy's President. I told her I had something important to say to him.

The very next day, I received a call from the President, who said, "I just had to speak to the person who made 20 calls to get to me." I told him why I called and what I thought that I could do to help Macy's, but, unfortunately, he was not very enthusiastic about my advice. Macy's went bankrupt one year later and maybe — just maybe — my advice could have kept that from happening. The moral of the story is that when you do not give in to your failures and persevere, you can achieve anything. Things will not work out every time, but if you keep giving yourself the opportunity to succeed, eventually you will.

3. Self-Reliant People Believe They Can Win

Self-reliant people have a strong will to achieve their goal. They have a spirit of never giving up. They are also confident about their capability to achieve their goals, so they prepare thoroughly to succeed

Imagine visiting one of your important clients to get a new business deal. If you prepare thoroughly, even if you are a little nervous, you still expect to win the contract. On the other hand, if you do not prepare enough to identify the real needs of your clients, you will lack confidence and expect to fail. An attitude like this guarantees your failure. This is why you need to strongly believe you can win and put in the time and effort to be well prepared.

Your biggest enemy is you. By teaching yourself to believe in your own success, you can achieve your goals again and again, exactly as you imagined. Below are ten credos that will help you continue to move toward your goals.

Ten Credos of the Harada Method:

1. How you work shows how you live your life.
2. Change yourself first before you try to change others.
3. Every tunnel has a light at the end.
4. Messiness messes up your mind. Cleaning cleans it.
5. Timing is money. Take action right now.
6. Who is your biggest enemy? It is YOU!
7. Always be positive!
8. Be a professional: Make a prediction and prepare to make it come true.
9. To succeed be strict, be gentle, and be funny.
10. Take time to reflect each day. Keep a diary.

4. Self-Reliant People Create Good Habits

Self-reliant people use a number of routines and habits each day to become successful. For example, at a large company in Tokyo, a businesswoman in her early 30s wakes up at 6:00am every morning to run 3 miles so that she can stay healthy. She cleans off her desk at the end of every day, so that in the morning when she arrives at work she can begin working immediately while her mind is fresh. Whenever she has to make a new proposal for a client, she has her secretary double-check the proposal, so that no typographical errors or omissions are left uncorrected. The woman regularly meets with friends after work to maintain a social life and keep her spirits uplifted.

These daily routines help the woman successfully perform her job. She has built effective habits to achieve her goals and succeed. She is careful to balance her life using these four aspects: spirit, skill, physical condition, and a daily routine (life).

In addition to focusing on her own life, the woman shows gratitude and respect to others on a daily basis. This is a key characteristic of self-reliant people. They help others understand what they are trying to achieve, because they know how important it is to receive help from others when pursuing their own goals.

5. Self-Reliant People are Reflective Thinkers

An important part of the Harada Method is to become more reflective thinkers. One way to do this is by writing your Harada Daily Diary every day. The act of writing helps you clarify your thoughts and keeps your mind and life organized. When you write, you pay more attention to the things that you should be thinking about.

Writing is also an effective way to learn new things.

Self-reliant people keep a diary in order to "record their memory" - to both summarize and reflect on daily experiences, and to also ensure that they are on the right path to attain their goals.

The Harada Diary is not like an ordinary diary. In an ordinary diary, you might write about your feelings or emotions, without any rules. The Harada Daily Diary gives you a framework to manage the process of pursuing your goals. You can use it to observe your life and ask questions, the same way a good coach would. In other words, the Diary allows you to become your own coach.

Writing is a Creative Act

It is not always easy to write - I know this from experience. Earlier in my life I was thoroughly convinced that I could not write at all. I simply believed what my teachers told me. Whenever I tried to write business letters, tears would come to my eyes; it was so bad. I remember hiring a secretary with a college degree in writing to help me write letters and memos. In a pivotal moment twelve years ago, I started to write articles and books. Miraculously, I overcame my resistance and wrote. It took me one year to write my first book "The Idea Generator," but I did it.

The more and more you write, the more clearly you begin to think. Writing stimulates your thinking process. Once you break through the resistance, the words just seem to flow out.

The Harada Diary helps you become a reflective

thinker and helps you organize the concrete steps needed to get closer to your goal.

6. Self-Reliant People Live in Harmony with the Four Aspects: Spirit, Skill, Physical Condition and a Daily Life

Self-reliant people coordinate their own life from the four aspects: spirit, skill, physical condition and a daily life. Almost everyone who lives in modern society lives under the influence of these four aspects.

When Harada started to coach at his school, he primarily focused on helping his students build their skills, but soon found that just building skills was not enough. The students had to believe in themselves. So Harada then focused on building skills and developing the right mindset.

This was an improvement, but the two aspects were not enough to develop real winners. Harada found that health and physical conditioning were equally important. Still, something was missing. It wasn't until he added the fourth aspect—"life"—that Harada's teams began to win gold medals. Harada found that when students added being helpful to others, the real power of his method came through.

Self-reliant people are adept at balancing the four aspects. They get a lot of energy from the four aspects and if all goes well, the aspects drive and motivate them. Self-reliant people manages their life by building a good relationship with their family and loved ones while achieving top job performance at the same time.

Remember, self-reliance is the ability to trust yourself to make the right decisions for your customer, for your organization, for society and for yourself. To be self-reliant, you must continuously improve your knowledge and continuously build up your skills, so that you can draw upon the highest part of yourself to make the right decisions. For me, most of my worst experiences occurred when I did not trust myself, the little voice inside, and ended up only listening to others.

Many years ago, I was going through basic training in Fort Dix, New Jersey. I was a new recruit in the US Army. During the first week, all 220 of us were standing in front of our captain when he said, "I need a typist. Who can type?" I was a pretty good typist, but I remembered what my friend, Ira, told me before going into the army. He said, "Norman, in the Army you never volunteer for anything." I thought that if I raised my hand, I would be stuck in a little room typing all day. One soldier finally raised his hand and said, "I can type with one finger." The captain said, "Well if that is all that is available to me, I will take you." So for the next eight weeks, I marched in the rain and crawled in the mud while the one finger guy sat in the captain's orderly room. It was a very important lesson for me - both to not trust Ira's advice and to be careful listening to other's advice and start trusting my own "gut." I wish I had known back then the Harada Method. I would have known to listen to my own instincts.

SUMMARY

"**If you are digging for oil, you must be sure that there is oil under the place you are digging.**" - Rudi[68]

At the end of July 2012, I was watching, with about a billion other people, the London Olympics on television. To me the Olympics are an example of what is possible if you create a clear goal and are willing to work very hard to attain that goal. Working towards the goal gives a strong meaning to your life and, achieving that goal is an amazing accomplishment.

A simple formula for success is:

$$D+G+W+P = S$$

D. Dream about what you feel you are able to do to be successful in life.
G. Set a clear goal on how to be the best at something.
W. Work towards that goal and believe in yourself
P. Plan, persevere and never give up.

S. Success is yours

Having now completed this book, you have tools in your hand for achieving your own personal success. As you've learned throughout the book the Harada Method is

---

[68] Rudi in 1971 to 1973 taught me Yoga meditation. The quote above tells me to make sure that when I set a goal and apply myself to attaining the goal, that the goal was actually achievable.

a sport's analogy based on what it takes to win at sports and to be able to apply the techniques both in your personal life and also in the workplace. I believe we all want to be winners, maybe we cannot all become Olympic winners, but surely you can dream about being the best at something; go after it and attain something wonderful in your life.

Mr. Harada has given you a proven method that has worked for thousands of people, and I am proud that I am able to share this incredible process with you. As you have seen through each chapter here is the complete step-by-step method Mr. Harada developed first for track and field athletes and then fine-tuned for industry. In this book you have been given each of the steps to follow to help you reach your goals. It is now up to you to pick your life goal and get started on your own journey towards working to achieve an amazing successful life. And remember even if it gets difficult, sometimes, never give up. Thousands of students and adults throughout Japan have new lives because they made the decision to follow the Harada Method. Now, reflect on what you read, dream what you really want to have a meaningful life, become an exceptional person, serve others well and go after it.

The Purposes of the Harada Method

- ∞ Teach managers to become leaders and coaches
- ∞ Help people develop their talents to their fullest
- ∞ Know how to pick successful goals
- ∞ Learn how to lead and motivate people to become high achievers
- ∞ Create a vision for long term personal success

SUMMARY

- Raise your self-esteem to help you achieve your vision
- How to work harder and better with more personal satisfaction when you have meaningful goals
- Learn and understand how to communicate better within your organization
- Improve your goal-setting technique
- Learn how to be an independent person and achieve personal and corporate goals
- Practice setting both long-term and short-term goals and objectives
- Know how to make decisions to benefit your organization, your customers and yourself
- Create a successful future
- Build your skills and be trusted for making decisions
- Repeatedly achieve success
- Understand what you need to do your job better and participate in your company's objectives
- Set up a mentor/mentee process in your organization
- Perfect your art to build your skills and capabilities
- Be the best you
- Enhance confidence
- Solve problems and make your work easier and more interesting
- Work toward your personal success
- Continually grow and build your skills
- Why you need a coach and what are the coach's basic skills
- Attain personal mastery
- Self-improvement with management's guidance
- Focus on value-adding activities and eliminate wasteful activities
- Create new habits to lead you to success

The Harada Method Steps are:

1 - Believe in Yourself
2 - Become Self-Reliant
3 - Determine the Key Service to Others
4 - Select Your Main Goal - The Long-Term Goal Setting Form
5 - Select Your Goals to Monitor Your Performance
6 - Set Milestone Goals
7 - State Your Purposes and Values
8 - Analyze Yourself
9 - Create Your 64-Chart with Eight Areas to Achieve Your Goal
10 - Write Eight Tasks for Each Aspect
11 - Write a Start Date for Each Task
12 - Select 10 Tasks to Get Started
13 - Build New Habits with New Routines
14 - Write Affirmations (Self-talk)
15 - Determine the Kind of Support You Need
16 - Select People to Support You
17 - Use Your Routine Check Sheet
18 - Keep a Daily Diary
19 - Work with a Coach/Mentor
20 - Revise the Monthly Long-Term Goal Setting Form

I want to thank Mr. Harada for allowing me to participate in this book and giving me the opportunity to teach his method. I wish you all great success.

INDEX

A3, 149
Accurate Machine & Tool Ltd., viii
Albert Einstein, 115
Andon, 225, 226, 234, 283, 324
Anthony, 92
APICS, 296, 325, 327
Big Indian, 145
Bill, vii, 235, 328
Bill Gates, 277
Bill Wootton, vii
Bob Nelson, 281
Book of Five Rings, 220
Bridgestone Tire, 265
Cambodia, 52
Canon, 4, 5, 196, 197, 199, 325
catchball, 262
Chase Manhattan Bank, 54
Chinese Proverb, 205
Christopher Marlowe, 299
Chugai Pharmaceuticals, 185
Confucius, 191, 233
Daily Management System, 4, 5
Day-to-day management by objectives, 4
Don Ephlin, 54

Dotonbori, 207, 209
Dover Corporation,, 191
Dr. Ellsbury, 29
Dr. Juran, 265, 324
Dr. Yoji Akao, 265
Eddie Robinson, 123
Edison, 156
Einstein, 155
Ernest Hemingway, 179
Florida Power & Light, 266
Ford Motor Company, 54
Gary Convis, 221
gemba, 223, 255
Gene Levine, ii, iii
General Electric, 3
General Motors, 224, 231, 265
George Halas, 139
Henry Ford, 195, 327
Hewlett-Packard, 266
Hino Motors, 181
Hokusetsu, 127, 128
Holiday Inns, 54
Hope Yen,, 68
Hoshin Planning, 149, 260, 261, 266, 267
Human Side of Lean, i, 6, 329
Humanity Improvement Workshop, 59
Intel, 266

Jack Caldwell, xxiv
Japanese Prime Minister Aso, 42
Japanese Union of Scientists and Engineers, 264
Jeremy Lin, 24, 131
Jidoka, 40
Jim Ryun, 146
Jim Swartz, 172
Joe Snyder, 53
John Harding, vii
John Schlee, 172
John Wooden, 87, 109
Joji Akao, xxii
Jonathan Puzzo, 66
Kaoru Ishikawa, 131, 259, 265
Kiichiro, 219, 220
Kirishima City, Kyushu, 201
Kokusan Denki, 199
Kokuyo, 203, 204
Komatsu Manufacturing, 265
Konosuke Matsushita, 101
Koshiro Sato, 163
Kyokutenho, 98
Kyowa, 203
Lee Kuan Yew, 193
Lehman Brothers, 41, 44
Lehman's, 137
Leonardo da Vinci, 156
Lexus, 133, 196, 197
LMI Aerospace Inc., vii

Lori Eberhardt, viii
Macy's, 309
Maguro, 201
Malcolm Gladwell, xxiv, 85
MAP, 1, 2, 3, 4, 5, 116
Mark Twain, 143
Matsumushi, 10, 31, 32, 47, 48, 59
Matsushita, 265
matsutake mushrooms, 52
MBO, 262, 265
Michael Jordan, 181
Michael Rose, 54
Midori Matsuoka, 113
Mikhail Baryshnikov, 149
Milbank Manufacturing, vii
Mr. Moriyuki, 207, 208, 209, 210
Mr. Nakamura, 1, 3, 4, 5, 202
Mr. Wada, 137
Ms. Sai, 137, 138
Musashi Miyamoto, 220
Neil Armstrong, 77
New York Knicks, 24, 131
Nichigai, 138
Nissan, 220
Noriko, 5, 6, 146
NUMMI, 224, 225
Ohno Circle, 219, 228
OJD, 240, 241
Okuda, 90, 127, 128

INDEX

Old Canon Production System, 4
Olympic Games, 46
PCDSS, 48, 299, 300, 302
PDCA, 254, 261, 264, 299
Peter Bodi, viii
Peter Ducker, 265
Phil Jackson, 91
Phillis, 55
poka-yoke, 2, 245, 324
Portland State University, 14, 68, 103, 328
President, 325, 326
President Kennedy, 77
Prius, 229, 230, 231
Procter & Gamble, 266
Productivity newsletter, 53
Randy Barnes, 79
Robert Miller, 183, 245
Round R" cycle, 254
Rudi, xix, 145
Ryan Allen, viii
Ryuji Fukuda, xxii, 327
Sakichi Toyoda, 219, 234
Samuel Johnson, 143
Samurai, 218, 220
Savand, 52
Shigehiro Nakamura, 1, 273, 327
Shigeo Shingo, xxi, 6, 121, 191, 278, 327, 329
Shingo Prize, vii, 183, 185, 192, 245, 246, 247, 248, 250, 256, 278, 326, 327
Singapore, 192, 193, 194

Six Sigma, 3, 229, 325, 326
SMED, 2, 103, 245, 324, 327
Standard Manpower, 2, 4
Stanley Lundine, 54
Steven Covey, xxiv
sumo, 98
supermeisters, 197
Tadashi Yanai, 40
Tahara, 110, 121, 136, 140, 196, 197
Taiichi Ohno, xxi, 6, 119, 191, 282, 327
Talisman Energy, viii
Temple Grandin, 52
Tommy Lasorda, 171
Toride, 196
Total Systems Development, viii, 259
Toyota, 40, 119, 133, 149, 193, 196, 197, 203, 215, 216, 217, 219, 220, 221, 222, 223, 224, 225, 226, 227, 229, 230, 231, 232, 233, 234, 235, 237, 239, 240, 241, 242, 243, 245, 248, 249, 265, 278, 281, 282, 283, 325, 327
Trace P. Tandy, vii
Uniqlo, 39, 40, 69, 89, 332
United Automobile Worker's union (UAW), 54
US Army, 314
US Synthetic, vii, 183, 191

Utah State University, 185, 326
Vince Lombardi, 37, 175
W. Edwards Deming, 135, 261

Xerox, 266
Yokogawa Electric, 193, 194

Author Biographies

Norman Bodek

It has been an amazing journey. In 1979, after 18 years working with data processing companies, I started Productivity Inc. and Productivity Press by first publishing a newsletter called PRODUCTIVITY. At the time, I knew virtually nothing about the subject of productivity and quality, and had spent very little time in manufacturing facilities, but I quickly became engrossed with the subject and went to Japan to discover the processes that were making them the world leader in quality improvement and productivity growth.

These past 33 years, I have visited Japan 80 times, visited over 250 plants and published over 100 Japanese management books in English (250 books in total), all without originally knowing a single person in Japan or speaking their language. A fortune cookie once told me, "You have the talent to discover the talent in others." That sums up my life. My claim to fame is finding the amazing people and tools, techniques and new thoughts that have revolutionized the world of manufacturing. Somehow, I met Dr. Deming, Dr. Juran, Phil Crosby, Dr. Ishikawa, Dr. Akao, Mr. Ohno, Dr. Shingo and a least 100 other great manufacturing masters. I was very fortunate to publish many of their books in English.

Each person I met gave me a new perspective on continuous improvement. Productivity Inc. was one of the first companies to publish books and training materials and to run conferences and seminars on Toyota Production System, (LEAN or JIT), SMED, CEDAC[69], quality control circles, 5S, visual factory, TPM, VSM, Kaizen Blitz, cell design, Poka-yoke, Lean accounting, Andon, Hoshin Kanri, Kanban, and Quick and Easy Kaizen.

As a presenter at conferences across the country and around the world, I like to share my journey and tell wonderful stories about the amazing people I met, what I

---

[69] CEDAC - Cause and Effect Diagram with the Addition of Cards, a technique that won Ryuji Fukuda the Deming Prize.

learned from them, and why that information is so vital to improving a company's performance.

My most powerful discovery was finding how Toyota, Canon and other Japanese companies brought out the infinite creative potential lying dormant inside every worker. When you unlock this hidden talent, people become highly motivated and actually love to come to work. Most recently, I have been working with Gulfstream Corporation, the private jet company, where 1000 people went from coming up with 16 implemented ideas per year in 2005 to over 35,000 in 2010. The ideas saved the company over $10,000,000 and have given the employees a new sense of pride in their work and in their lives. Now with my new discovery of the Harada Method, it continues my work of bringing the most out of people to reach individual and organizational goals.

Education: University of Wisconsin, New York University (BA), New York University Graduate School of Business, and New York University College of Education

Instructor: American Management Associations, Control Data Institute, President Regan's Productivity Conference - Washington, DC, PPORF Conference - Japan, Total Productive Maintenance Conference - Tokyo, Institute of Industrial Engineers, American Society for Quality, APICS, Productivity, Inc. Conferences and Seminars, Dresser Mfg., Union Carbide, AVCO Corporation, Larsen & Turbo - India, Productivity - Madras (Chennai), India, London - England, Jutland - Denmark, Plastics Industry in Ireland, Six Sigma conferences and many more.

Recipient of the Shingo Prize* for Manufacturing Excellence and also created the Shingo Prize with Dr. Vern Buehler sponsored by Utah State University, and received the Six Sigma Global Grand medal from ICBUPR.

Professional Career: Public Accountant and Insurance Broker, Vice President Data Utilities, New York City, and Barbados, West Indies, President Key Universal Ltd. with offices in Greenwich, Connecticut and Grenada, West Indies.

1979-1999 Started Productivity, Inc. & Productivity Press with offices in Norwalk, Connecticut and Portland, Oregon.

Newsletters: PRODUCTIVITY, Total Employee Involvement (TEI), The Service Insider, Quick Change Over (QCO), Total Productive Maintenance (TPM) and Perfect Customer Service.

Study missions to Japan: led around 35 missions visiting 250 manufacturing plants.

Conferences: Ran over 100 conferences on productivity and quality improvement including Productivity The American Way, Best of America, Quality, Quality Service, TPM, and TEI

Seminars: Held hundreds of seminars on TPM, TQM, TEI, QCO, Visual Management, 5S, JIT and others.

---

*For information on the prize:
http://www.shingoprize.org/shingo/index.html

In-Plant Training Events: Five Days and One Night (now called Kaizen Blitz), Maintenance Miracle, Quick Changeovers, Visual Factory, 5S and benchmark plant visits and seminars with American Manufacturing companies.

Books Published: Taiichi Ohno - Toyota Production System (JIT), Henry Ford - Today and Tomorrow, A New American TQM, Yoji Akao - Quality Function Deployment (QFD) and Hoshin Kanri, Dr. Ryuji Fukuda - Managerial Engineering, CEDAC and Building Organizational Fitness, Dr. Shigeo Shingo's - Toyota Production System, SMED, Poka-Yoke, Non-Stock Production, Shigeichi Moriguchi - Software Excellence, Shigeru Mizuno - Management for Quality Improvement (The 7 New QC Tools), Seiichi Nakajima - Total Productivity Maintenance (TPM), Michel Greif - The Visual Factory, Ken'ichi Sekine - One Piece Flow, Shigehiro Nakamura - The New Standardization, and many other books on world-class manufacturing and total quality management.

1990 - Called "Mr. Productivity" by Industry Week

1999 - Started PCS Inc. - Press with a monthly newsletter, consulting, and workshops on Quick and Easy Kaizen and Improving Customer Service.

2001 - Called "Mr. Lean" in Quality Progress Magazine

2007 - 2012 - Keynoted dozens of management conferences throughout America, Malaysia, Mexico, Canada, Ireland and Great Britain and also for FAA, IIE, ASQ, BAE, DCAA, APICS, WCBF, Lean Accounting Summit, TBM, Shingo Prize, AME, MEP, Iowa Quality,

Sandia Labs, CME Winnipeg Lean Conference, AME Conferences, etc.

2010 - 2012 Adjunct professor at Portland State University teaching the Best of Japanese Management and the Harada Method, and also taught at the Monterrey Institute of Technology.

Inducted into Industry Week's Manufacturing Hall of Fame

Books written:

> **The Idea Generator - Quick and Easy Kaizen**
> Co-authored with Bunji Tozawa
> PCS Press 2001
>
> **The Idea Generator - Workbook**
> PCS Press 2002
>
> **Kaikaku: The Power and Magic of Lean**
> PCS Press 2004
>
> **All You Gotta Do Is Ask**
> Co-authored with Chuck Yorke
> PCS Press 2005
>
> **Rebirth of American Industry**
> Co-authored with Bill Waddell
> PCS Press 2005
>
> **How to Do Kaizen**
> PCS Press 2009

The Harada Method - The Spirit of Self-Reliance - The Human Side of Lean
Co-authored with Takashi Harada

Books edited and published:

JIT Is Flow
Hiroyuki Hirano and Makoto Furuya
PCS Press 2006

The Handbook for Idea Generation - The Scientific Thinking Mechanism
Dr. Shigeo Shingo
PCS Press 2008

Fundamental Principles of Lean Manufacturing
Dr. Shigeo Shingo
PCS Press 2009

Articles published in:

Quality Digest Magazine
Solutions - IIE Magazine
Target - Association for Manufacturing Excellence (AME)
Quality World
The Journal for Quality and Participation
T + D Magazine - ASTD
Manufacturing Engineering - SME's magazine
Timely Tips for Teams - monthly
NWLean
HR.COM
Superfactory.com

Over 100 articles published in the last seven years.

Radio - ran a management interview program in New England.

E-learning - course developed with Society of Manufacturing Engineers, MEP.

Takashi Harada

Takashi Harada developed his Harada Method from his experience as a track and field coach. He has since taught the Harada Method to more than 55,000 people at over 280 companies. He has published 11 books in Japan, this book, his 12th, is his first in English.

Takashi Harada was a junior high school track and field coach in the worst neighborhood of Osaka, Japan. The school where Mr. Harada worked was the lowest rated of Osaka's 380 schools. The neighborhood children had very little confidence in themselves and even less hope for their futures. Mr. Harada did not accept the poor attitude among his students, and he set out to change it, using sports to improve their mindset.

Mr. Harada noticed that there were other coaches in Osaka that consistently had great teams. He studied those coaches and other great leaders throughout the world and put together a methodology to help his students be successful in life. Mr. Harada's winning method guided his students to win 13 gold medals in the national track and field competition. For the students, this was like winning the Olympics - they were the best athletes in all of Japan. His school was rated number one in track and field for six years in a row, and the entire student body raised its academic performance as well.

His last school went from the worst rated Junior High School in track and field to number one out of 380 schools, and has sustained being number one for ten years even after Mr. Harada left the school. The Harada Method worked and is continuing to work.

After 20 years as a coach, Mr. Harada took his method to industry and his clients include Mitsubishi Financial Services, UniQlo, Kirin Beer and many others. He currently teaches throughout Japan:

1. How to be an ideal leader
2. How to build effective groups
3. How to improve work performance

Takashi Harada graduated from Nara University of Education.

Professional Career:

1982-2003
Worked as a public junior high school physical education teacher. Produced 13 gold medals, No.1 in Japan in track and field.

2003-
CEO of Harada Education Institute, Inc. Worked as an instructor of employee training at many leading companies in Japan, such as UniQlo, Kanebo Cosmetics, Nomura Holdings, Kirin Beverage, Chugai Pharma Manufacturing, and many other listed companies.

2010-
Professor of Faculty of Business Management at Business Breakthrough University (online university), teaching "How to coach yourself to be self-reliant"

Seminars: Has run over 50 seminars on the Harada Method (goal-setting and how to grow self-reliant people)

In-Plant Training Events:
Working with over 280 companies during the past 9 years, including: Nomura Holdings, UniQlo, Kanebo Cosmetics, Chugai Pharma Manufacturing, Kirin Beverage, Mitsubishi UFJ Morgan Stanley, Takeda Pharmaceutical Company, Janssen Pharmaceutical, Osaka Gas, and many other leading companies.

Training for Teachers:
Holds free seminars for school teachers with over 2300 attending these seminars.

Books written:

Children won't change if they do not have a whole-hearted education 2003

Education that always wins 2003

Textbook for success 2005

How to make your dream absolutely come true (with DVD) 2005

Lifestyle guidance for adults to change 2006

60-day workbook 2007

A charismatic teacher's heart cultivation 2008

Takashi Harada's Cram School for success (with DVD) 2008

64 Passionate words 2010

Things to convey to children now 2010

Self-praising ability for resilient heart 2011

The Harada Method – The Spirit of Self-Reliance - The Human Side of Lean
Co-authored with Norman Bodek

TV Appearance – appears on many popular TV programs including: "Gaia no Yoake" " Jonetsu Tairiku" "Shin-Houdou 2001" "Kin-suma"

As Harada explains his goals for the works he does:

"One of my current goals is to eliminate bullying from schools and prevent children from committing suicide

Another goal is, as always, to multiply the number of self-reliant people and self-reliant companies in Japan and in the world, to contribute to the improvement and realization of world peace."

Read more about Takashi Harada (in Japanese) at his website: http://www.harada-educate.jp.

Printed in Dunstable, United Kingdom